MW01268203

Brain
Slice

An Introduction to
Psychological Neuroscience

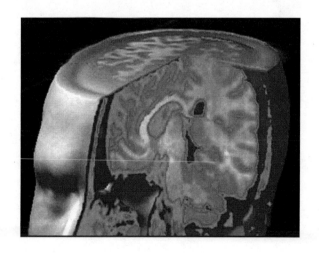

Bruce H. Hinrichs

Copyright © 2011 by Bruce H. Hinrichs

All rights reserved. No part of this book may be reproduced, stored, or transmitted
in any form or manner without prior written permission of the publisher
with the exception of brief quotations in critical articles or reviews.

Printed in the United States of America

Front cover image © Scott Camazine, used with permission
Back cover image © Bruce H. Hinrichs

ISBN: 978-0-9790129-3-8
0-9790129-3-7

Ellipse Publishing Company
225 Groveland Avenue
Minneapolis, Minnesota 55403

What is the verdict of the vastest mind?
Silence: the book of fate is closed to us.
Man is a stranger to his own research;
He knows not whence he comes, nor whither goes.
Tormented atoms in a bed of mud,
Devoured by death, a mockery of fate.
But thinking atoms, whose far-seeing eyes,
Guided by thought, have measured the faint stars,
Our being mingles with the infinite;
Ourselves we never see, or come to know.

A caliph once, when his last hour had come,
This prayer addressed to him he reverenced:
"To thee, sole and all-powerful king, I bear
What thou dost lack in thy immensity—
Evil and ignorance, distress and sin."
He might have added one thing further — hope.

– Excerpts from *Poem on the Lisbon Disaster* (1756) by Voltaire

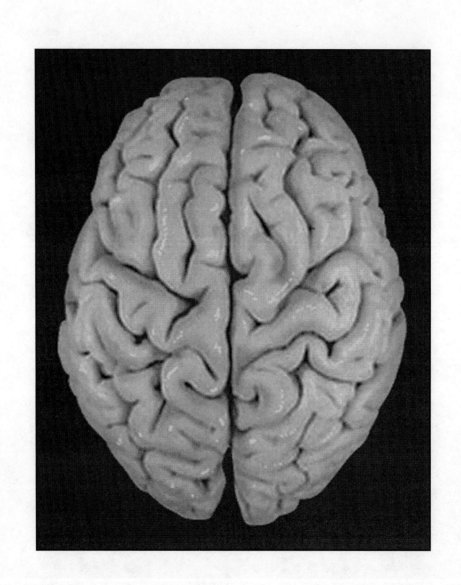

Table of Contents

Chapter 1

INTRODUCTION
Just what is a brain, anyway?

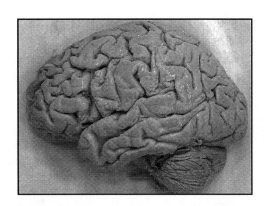

It's funny, but still today, after all these years, I remember and quite often think about a silly black and white movie that I saw when I was about 10 years old. It sticks in my mind so vividly because it was the first time I saw a human brain. It was scary! I don't know why it is frightening for children to see a brain, but it is. Seeing a brain outside the body, all wrinkly and gooey and mysterious, *is* scary, but it is also utterly, incredibly humbling and captivating. It definitely gets you thinking. Yes, that's right – brains get you thinking!

A brain is an organ in your head. But, what exactly is a brain? What is it made of, how does it develop, how does it work, what influences it, and what are the secrets of its functioning? These, as you are well aware, are some of the most mind-boggling issues that today fascinate the general public and brain scientists, alike.

Brain Interface

Hippocampus, which is Greek for "seahorse," is the name of a part of the brain that curls around deep behind the ears. The hippocampus is critically important for learning and memory, and is often damaged by stroke or diseases such as Alzheimer's. Scientists, led by Theodore Berger, working with laboratory rats have created an implantable silicon microchip that can reproduce functions of part of the hippocampus (Graham-Rowe, 2004a). When electrodes record signals from the rat's hippocampus and send them to the microchip, the output of the chip matches the natural signals emitted from a slice of hippocampal tissue. The device is only 2mm square and within several years may be ready for implantation in human hippocampi.

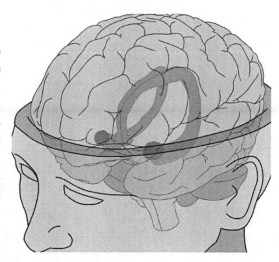

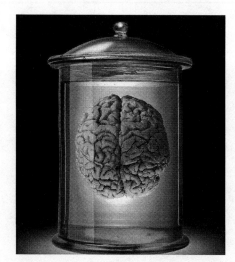

The brain of a lamprey eel is sitting in a jar at Northwestern University in Chicago. Remarkably, that eel brain is controlling the movements of a small robot on wheels (Mussa-Ivaldi, 2000). The eel's brain sits in a cold, oxygen-rich saline solution, and has two sets of wires connected to it, one set coming in and one going out. The brain receives electrical signals from light sensors on the robot, and, in turn, sends electrical signals to the wheels of the robot. The eel brain moves the robot toward the light if the wires are placed in a certain part of the brain, away from the light if the wires are placed in a different part of the brain, and moves the robot in circles if the wires are placed in yet another part of the eel brain. This is the first time that two-way communication has been successful between a brain and a machine.

Just as amazing, scientists at Duke University Medical Center recently were able to move a robot's arm via a signal sent from a computer 600 miles away at the Massachusetts Institute of Technology. But get this: The computer was programmed using the signals from a monkey's brain to its arm! Electrodes recorded the impulses from the monkey's brain to its arm, the signal was fed into a computer, and then sent to Duke University where the electrical signal was sent to a robot. The robot's arm moved just as the monkey's arm had (Nicolelis, 2001).

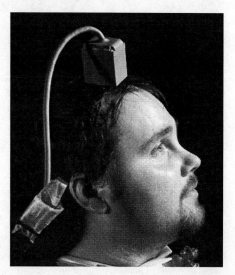

In a similar experiment in Philadelphia, electrodes were placed into a rat's brain and connected by wires to a robot arm. When the rat is thirsty it can move the robot arm via electrical signals sent from its brain, and the robot brings water to the rat. The rat's brain is controlling the movements of the robot (Chapin, 2001). Researchers also have fitted a monkey with a brain-machine interface that allows him to control a robot with his thoughts (Carmena, 2003). Also, a rat with electrodes implanted in brain areas that control behavior allows researchers to remotely control movement of the rat (Talwar, 2002). Such research could lead to remote controlled rats that could be guided to enter buildings or defuse bombs. Could humans be fitted with such electrodes? Naturally, experts in the new field of **neuroethics** are concerned with such issues.

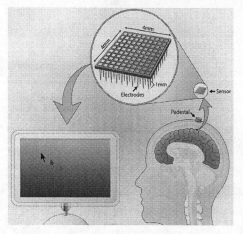

But some humans already are fitted with such electrodes. For example, people who are paralyzed are able to move a computer cursor just by thinking via wires implanted in their brains. The wires are connected to computers. When the people think about moving, the computer cursor moves on the screen. Obviously, such advances could help many paralyzed people. This particular system is called **BrainGate** and is an example of a **brain-computer interface** (BCI), a direct communication pathway between a brain and an external device used to help people with damaged cognitive or sensory-motor functions. A commercial BCI device, Intendix, allows a patient with locked-in syndrome to signal a computer by using his or her brain waves detected by an EEG cap. There are several such **neuroprosthetics** under development, including one that will automatically move electrodes in the brain seeking out the strongest signals (Graham-Rowe, 2004b).

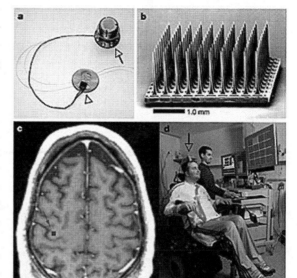

In another strange case of new technology, Kevin Warwick, a Professor of Cybernetics in England, has a chip implanted in his arm that can turn on and off lights, open doors, and allow his computer to track his movements. He said, "I did begin to feel strangely connected to both the building and the computer." He wants to implant a chip in his wife's arm and transmit information between them via the computer, and then to eventually implant a similar chip in his brain

How long will it be before many of us have our brains linked to computers, and what will this technology allow us to do? I'll bet you can think of lots of wild possibilities for such scenarios – from science fiction to practical applications. It sounds like something out of *Star Trek*, but it is happening right now in neurobiology research. In fact, author, inventor, and futurist **Raymond Kurzweil** believes we are very near **singularity** – a time when technological advancements and an intelligence explosion will make life qualitatively different and hard to predict, artificial intelligence will surpass the capacity of the human brain, and humans will transcend biology. A singularity summit has been held each year since 2006. Perhaps one day we will download our minds into something like a computer disk, and in a sense become immortal. Would you do it?

Brains as Computers

Inside your head is a three-pound computer, one of the most powerful computers in the world. The three pounds are mostly water; in fact, less than one pound consists of living cells. These brain cells – **neurons** – use electrical and chemical activity to compute your emotions, thoughts, decisions, moods, memories, and behaviors. Oh, and tonight when you go to sleep, your three-pound computer will create your dreams.

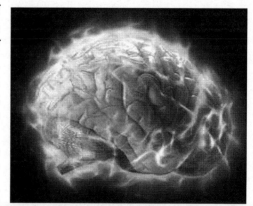

For centuries, philosophers have puzzled over the mind-body problem, the captivating enigma that asks how subjective mental states are connected to our objective physical biology. In recent years, neuroscientists have made spectacular achievements in describing the cellular and molecular actions of the nervous system while cognitive psychologists have indirectly observed and measured mental and psychological functions, sometimes with ingenious experimental methodology, and often borrowing brain imaging techniques from neuroscience.

The most recent contributors to the mind-body problem are computer network experts who study how individual elements interact in a systematic way producing computational processes that give rise to information processing and artificial intelligence. Pioneers such as Alan Turing, John von Neumann, Warren McCulloch and Walter Pitts, and more recently

Patricia Churchland and Terrence Sejnowski have provided an analysis of systems at a higher level than the typical biomedical approaches of neuroscience and at a lower level than the macro states and behaviors favored by psychologists. By examining **neural networks**, these researchers hope to uncover just how individual cells combine to create emergent phenomena that are more than the sum of their parts.

Of course, in each case the attention is on the human brain as the locus of mental and psychological functions. Computer guru and artificial intelligence pioneer Marvin Minsky has called the brain a "meat machine" and a machine that "clanks softly." Taking

this concept of the brain as a soft computational machine allows for an interesting commentary on the chess match between Garry Kasparov and the IBM computer sometimes called **Deeper Blue** (because it is an improved version of Deep Blue beaten by Kasparov the previous year). In this view it was not man against machine as much as it was one type of machine – or process, if you prefer – against another. As was shown, one process happens to be better at chess than the other. Deeper Blue was victorious.

Critics complain that a digital computer lacks awareness or understanding, that it is *just* making unconscious computations. But a brain is a type of computer and it has awareness and understanding. A brain also *just* makes unconscious computations – by neurons creating electrical energy and squirting transmitter chemicals. This, of course, is the essential mystery: How can these singularly objective cellular brain events transform into psychological states, moods, and behaviors? The consciousness we experience apparently is achieved via the interaction of billions of unconscious computational events, which in themselves have no awareness or understanding.

Certainly Deeper Blue was made and programmed by humans, but so was Kasparov! If we're giving credit to Deeper Blue's programmers, then let's give credit to the programmers of Kasparov: his genes, parents, teachers, previous opponents, authors of books he read, etc. Also, some machines today are made by other machines, and someday computers will likely be made and programmed by other computers. So what? None of these truths diminishes human integrity, dignity, or worth. There is no threat. Brains are better at some things, while silicon digital computers excel at others.

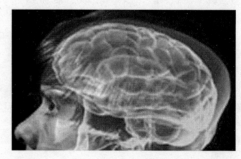

Analogies

Years ago we were told that a human brain functions like a telephone switchboard. Some people still remember the scratchy 16mm movies shown in elementary school that illustrated brain activity as a sequence of switchboard plugs being methodically pulled from and inserted into an impressive array of holes. This analogy was readily embraced throughout society, in and out of schools, and it even sprouted in pedestrian places such as the silly 1972 Woody Allen movie, *Everything You Always Wanted To Know About Sex, But Were Afraid To Ask.* Allen showed the brain as a command center for body actions (sex, in this case), that were initiated and regulated via telephone communication.

The days when a brain was likened to a telephone switchboard are thankfully long gone. In the modern Zeitgeist, the idea seems humorously antiquated, belonging more properly to an era of bobby-soxers, air raid drills, and bomb shelters. But contemporary

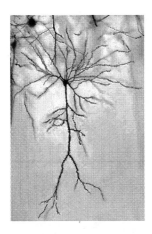

society need not go metaphor-less, for, as is usually the case, when one analogy grows passe, another elbows its way into our collective hearts. The au courant brain metaphor, which is both ubiquitous and appropriate for the "information age," is that a brain is like a computer.

Our popular culture absorbs and reflects this analogy regularly through TV characters such as Commander Data of *Star Trek: The Next Generation*, who achieves consciousness with a "positronic" electronic matrix brain, through TV newscasts that regularly report research findings that certain human traits are "hard-wired" into our brains, and through movies such as *Brainstorm* (1983), *Total Recall* (1990), *Until the End of the World* (1991), *AI* (2001), *I, Robot* (2004), and so many others that envision machines that are able to interface with living human brains and thereby access various mental functions, such as memories and dreams. Apparently, the brain-computer analogy is widespread and implicitly accepted throughout our culture. The brain has gone cyber.

Is a Brain Like a Computer?

When first proposed in the 1960s, the brain-computer analogy was widely criticized, quite unfairly, on the basis that brains do very different tasks than do computers. For example, it was noted that a brain is exquisitely excellent at visually recognizing a face or an object, while a computer is clunky and exceedingly slow at pattern recognition. On the other hand, a computer can do complex mathematical calculations at extremely high speed, while a brain is stumped by such tasks. While these indeed were, and still are, accurate observations, what makes this criticism a red herring is that it isn't the particular content of a computation that determines if something is like a computer, rather, it is the process used; it isn't *what* is done, it's *how* it's done that matters.

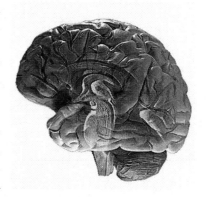

A more valid complaint of the brain-computer analogy regards the word *like*. The brain is not *like* a computer; it *is* a computer! Certainly a brain does not compute the same information that a PC does, but in the method – the manner in which it processes information – the brain is computing. A brain is a computer, but a very different sort than we are used to. For better or worse, your brain is a computer. Greetings, Data!

This concept is widely accepted among cognitive neuroscientists including philosophers Paul Churchland and Patricia Smith Churchland who recently wrote, "The brain is a kind of computer, although most of its properties remain to be discovered. Characterizing

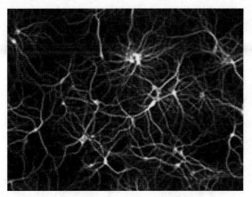

the brain as a kind of computer is neither trivial nor frivolous. The brain does compute functions, functions of great complexity, but not in the classical artificial intelligence fashion.

When brains are said to be computers, it should not be implied that they are serial, digital computers, that they are programmed, that they exhibit the distinction between hardware and software or that they must be symbol manipulators or rule followers. Brains are computers in a radically different style."

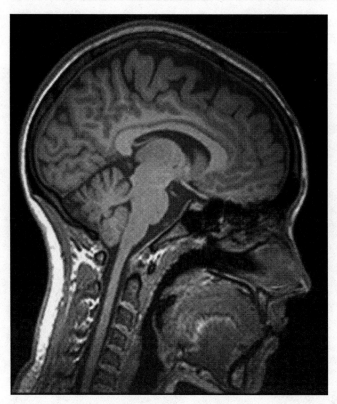

What seems clear is that, whatever other qualities it may possess, a brain appears to be a kind of computer, a nature-made computer. Through a series of complex interactions, a brain takes incoming sensory signals, processes that information, and achieves a computational product, an output. Think of your senses as the keyboard or modem, and your conscious mind as the monitor. Danish science writer Tor Norretranders (1998) suggests just this analogy: brain = computer, and mind = monitor. The output of the brain includes regulation of body systems and emotions, behaviors, and thoughts, both conscious and unconscious. A brain does compute. Of course, exactly *what* it computes varies significantly from a PC or Macintosh.

This idea is typically a frightening one to many people, though not to a majority of brain researchers who have calmly accepted it, at least at some fundamental level despite disagreements over nuances. For our part, although we may have some trepidation, if we are willing to take an open-minded view, then it seems reasonable, even fun, to agree with the experts that a brain is a natural computer, the world's first computer, the best and brightest computer. There should be nothing threatening or dehumanizing about this view. In fact, adopting this insight may help us to better understand and accept emotional, behavioral, and cognitive differences between people and the mental problems that beset us. However, even if we accept this framework, significant clarifications are necessary lest unwarranted conclusions be drawn.

What Kind of Computer Do You Have?

A brain may be a computer, but it is a distinctly different sort of computer from the silicon chip models on our desks. The complex networking that is characteristic of both a PC and a brain is achieved in each case through the use of entirely different substances and different systems of organization. First, and most obvious, the cells (neurons) that permit communication within a brain are *alive*. A brain is a living computer. Unlike a typical Mac or PC, a brain consists of cells that are alive, cells that are to some extent self-organizing rather than organized by algorithms, and cells that operate in multiple circuits independently of other circuits. A brain can do many tasks at once; it is not a serial computer. A brain is a massive parallel processing computer made of self-organized, living tissue; Not the same thing at all as the computers we know.

Brain cells are not silicon chips or transistors. Neurons, like all cells, require oxygen and involve complex biological processes that are driven by genetic codes. Cells are subject to malfunctions, irregularities, and damage via biological mechanisms (consider, for

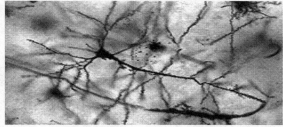

example, **Alzheimer's disease**). This simple realization leads us to the most enlightening fact that since brain cells are alive and therefore are malleable and dynamic, it becomes difficult, perhaps impossible, to distinguish between hardware and software within the brain.

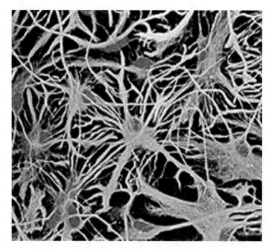

In contrast, a semiconductor computer uses cells that are essentially static, unchanged by the signals they carry. In a PC or Mac, the hardware is not significantly altered by the software program it runs. When the software is removed, the hardware is unchanged, back to normal, ready for more software. Brains don't work like that. A brain's hardware is pivotally changed by its software – a process that is at the heart of how a brain stores information (that is, remembers) and maintains continuity. As a brain takes in information through the senses, the cells that compose the hardware are physically changed by the process.

Take language, for example. One brain may run an English program, while another runs French. Each brain has been programmed through experience, and the software programs are now integral parts of the hardware of the brain. The hardware of each brain is importantly different from the other at a cellular level. They are different in a physical/chemical way that would be extremely difficult, if not impossible, to undo without doing damage to their structures. In a brain, the software is intricately intertwined with the hardware. The program (in this example, language) cannot be removed without altering the hardware. Even while asleep (and not dreaming), when one's conscious mind is "turned off," the nature of the software programs is retained within the hardware so that when one awakes, the same old memories, thoughts, and feelings are booted up and running.

Make Up Your Mind!

This insight may lead us to wonder what exactly it is about brains that allows them to create thoughts, memories, awareness, emotions – that is, a mind. Where in the brain's biological processes are the key elements that give us consciousness? Are mental and emotional experiences a product of the brain's cellular interactions, and therefore perhaps reproducible using inorganic networks that replicate brain networks? Or, are conscious experiences dependent on the biological characteristics of brain cells themselves? Does a mental experience, such as seeing, hearing, or feeling, depend on some particular quality of the individual cells of the brain (the neurons), or, is the computational interaction between the cells (the networks) sufficient to produce awareness?

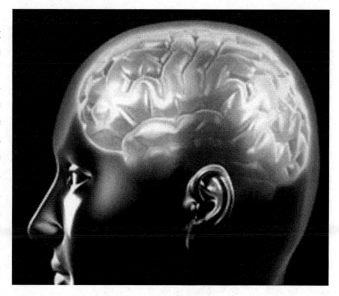

If it is the brain cells that are crucial for creating consciousness, then we may wonder which specific properties or characteristics of the cells are the necessary ones. Do other cells that have those properties then also have a mental life? Could mental experiences be replicated in a laboratory by reproducing those special cellular characteristics?

On the other hand, if mental experiences are not produced by particular aspects of the cells, but instead by their interacting networks doing some sort of computing (the viewpoint of **connectionists**), then it should be possible to build a machine that could generate mental

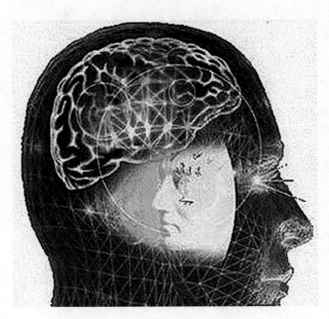

phenomena. If a silicon chip computer was built to exactly simulate brain connections, would it not feel? If not, then why not? What would be missing?

Of course, it is entirely possible – in fact, it is entirely likely – that the creation of mental and emotional experiences depends on a unique combination of cellular characteristics and their interactions, that both biological cellular mechanisms and neural networks are necessary. In that event, it would take information about both neural networks and cell biology to understand, and to artificially create, a conscious mind.

When a brain creates a mind, when thoughts and emotions are formed by brain properties, states, conditions, or actions, then precisely what are the particular, distinctive elements involved? Are thinking, feeling, dreaming, and consciousness unique to humans, or are these subjective experiences shared on some continuum with animals, insects, amoebae, perhaps even inorganic materials? In other words, are mental phenomena reproducible? Could a non-living machine, if properly constructed, conceivably conceive a thought, feel, think, dream?

A Scientific Answer

When we ask how it is that a brain creates a mind, it is somewhat similar to asking how any observed quality is created by its physical constituents; for example, how is it that rocks are hard, iron is magnetic, ice is cold, or for illustrative purposes, how water creates wetness? Just as wetness is a property or quality of water, so the mind is a property or quality of the brain. Wetness is a state or condition that is created by the physical nature of water, and similarly we can conceptualize mental experiences as states or conditions created by the physical nature of the brain. Although this is not a perfect comparison – in fact there are no perfect comparisons since a mind is the only thing we know to have awareness – still we can use this comparison to help us achieve a better conceptual paradigm of the mind-brain connection.

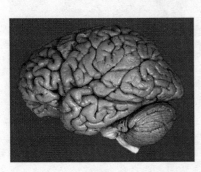

When we attempt to explain a certain phenomenon, a *scientific* answer is one that describes the physical/chemical properties and interactions underlying the quality to be explained. For example, wetness is a quality that is scientifically explained by reference to certain properties and interactions of hydrogen and oxygen atoms. Employing this paradigm, mental experiences can similarly be scientifically explained by detailing the specific brain substances and activities that generate them. Since the mind is one of the things that a brain does – when brain cells are in a certain state or network – a scientific explanation of the mind would thus consist of a detailed description of the physical/chemical brain states and networks associated with each mental experience.

Though most people find this form of answer acceptable for explaining other phenomena, it is typically found unsatisfactory for the question of how a brain creates a mind, since people want an answer of a different sort, one invoking the metaphysical or supernatural. Although the scientific approach may seem inadequate, it *is* how we explain other phenomena, and in those cases, it is accepted. We don't ask how it is that water creates wetness; the *how* doesn't make sense, other than by explaining wetness with reference to its underlying physical features. Perhaps this is the best approach to understanding the mind: to reduce mental experiences to their

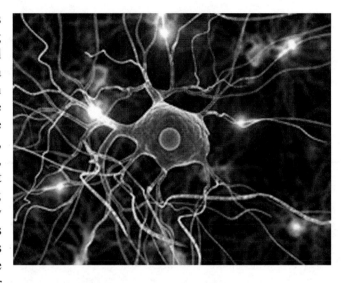

underlying physical features and not ask *how* it is that these features produce the mind, that is, not ask for supernatural or metaphysical explanations. Such answers are inexplicable within the language of science but may be appropriate to poetry, philosophy, or the arts, fields that offer fundamentally different ways of thinking about these issues.

Basics of Brain and Mind

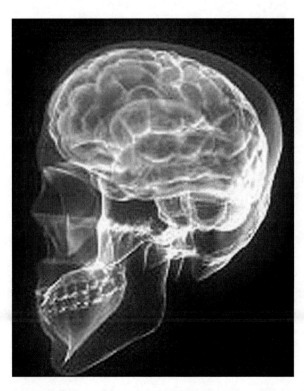

The brain is a physical thing within the natural world, not a supernatural or metaphysical entity. Minds are not supernatural entities, but are personal experiences produced when brains are in a state of awareness of their own functioning, most probably a state created through the complex intercommunication between and among brain sub-computers for vision, hearing, language, attention, and other sensory, cognitive, and perceptual functions. Minds are not substances; they are subjective experiences that the brain creates as a window into certain aspects of its own functioning. A brain, or a particular sub-division of the brain, is able to create an awareness of certain of its own states or functions – a kind of self-monitoring.

This concept of the mind may help us in speculating about why the mind exists. Why didn't a brain evolve without consciousness? What was the evolutionary impetus for the development of awareness? Viewing mental experiences as self-monitoring events helps us initiate some hypotheses about why consciousness would have evolutionary survival advantages over a non-conscious brain.

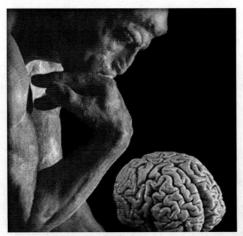

Although some experts have proposed that minds and brains are the same (in fact, some writers have recently begun to use the term "brain-mind"), minds are *not* brains any more than wetness is water. Minds are a quality or product of certain brain activity, one of the many things that a brain does, along with control of muscles, organs, and body housekeeping functions. While one is asleep, for example, a brain can be performing many functions, although consciousness (the mind) is temporarily turned off. Incidentally, the question of how a brain creates consciousness is becoming a legitimate research subject. The popular idea that conscious decisions are made in a non-physical mind and then transferred to the brain now seems quaintly far-fetched.

In an insightful experiment, **Benjamin Libet** (1985) attempted to measure the exact moment when a person makes a mental decision. Libet measured brain electrical activity while subjects were asked to make simple decisions about moving their arms. Libet found consistent, regular brain signals occurring just *prior* to a person's awareness of making a conscious decision. That is, brain cells were firing in the area of the brain that controls arm movements *before* subjects had a conscious awareness of making a decision to move their arms. This finding is puzzling if we accept the folk psychology notion that conscious decisions are not physical in nature but are mystical, non-brain events that direct behavior. But whence cometh the mental decision, if not from the brain? How could a mental or emotional state, an awareness of any kind, possibly be created without some prior, corresponding brain activity? It should not seem surprising that brain activity precedes mental awareness – in fact it must! Where else could conscious awareness come from? Choice is a brain event.

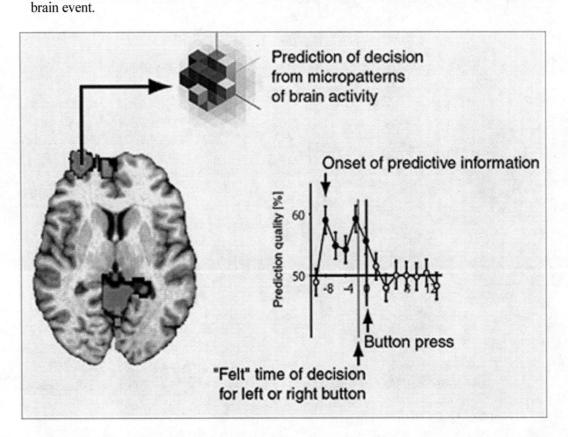

Philosopher **Daniel Dennett**, in his book *Consciousness Explained* (1991), has noted that Libet's study harbors an even more obscure notion of folk psychology: that conscious decision-making takes place at a particular, specific moment in time. Dennett argues that consciousness is an on-going process that has no specific moment of occurrence because there is no central location in the brain where it occurs. Dennett quite rightly points out that there is no such "Cartesian Theatre," as he calls it, in the brain that "watches" or "looks" at brain functioning and then accordingly derives or creates a mental awareness or consciousness. There is no singular part of the brain that acts as watcher or consciousness. That is a popular illusion with neither rhyme nor reason. There is no empirical evidence of such a thing, nor does the idea seem reasonable or logical.

Our Journey

A brain has many tasks. One of the most interesting is the creation of thoughts, feelings, dreams, choices, personal identity, and awareness of the environment and the self – in other words, a conscious mind. The specific details of how the mind is created by the brain are yet to be unraveled and are likely to be complex and difficult to uncover and elucidate. Still, there is no reason to believe that these details are conceptually any more inaccessible to scientific investigation and scrutiny than any other complex phenomenon. Nor is there any reason to feel threatened or dehumanized by such studies. In fact, people who scientifically study the mind are demonstrating a central focus of humanism: a high regard for understanding human nature and experience without supernatural biases. One thing on which it is easy to agree is that how the brain creates the mind is one of the most fascinating and exhilarating of all questions.

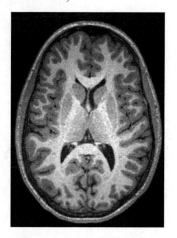

As you read these words, consider for a moment the idea that an abundance of intricate electrical and chemical signals surging through your brain at this very moment is responsible right now for your awareness and attention, your seeing and understanding, your memories and emotions, your questions, concerns, and doubts, your creative impulses, curiosity and emerging ideas, and any excitement you may now feel as the living brain-computer in your head invites you to explore its cyber space, to delve into the mysteries of the human brain and mind, to take a journey into psychological neuroscience. Happy computing!

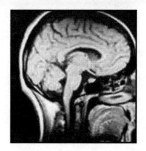

Chapter 2

HISTORY OF BRAIN
Wild notions and wacky tinkering!

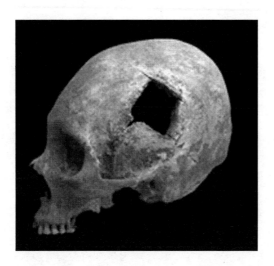

Brains have been of interest to peoples of many cultures for thousands of years. The first recorded reference to the brain appeared in a papyrus written in hieroglyphics nearly 4000 years ago. The papyrus described two patients who had been wounded in the head and experienced various mental and physical ailments.

Clues from prehistory indicate that people were interested in the brain even before there was writing. For example, the technique of **trephining** or **trepanning** – pounding a hole in a person's head, ostensibly to cure some malady or to release evil spirits – was performed in many cultures before the advent of writing. Archaeologists have unearthed skulls from preliterate civilizations with rough holes in them, apparently pounded into the skull with a sharp rock. Some of the skulls show signs of healing, so the "patients" must have survived the procedure.

During the Middle Ages (5th–15th c.), such operations were fairly common. A drill-like instrument known as a "trepan" was used in an attempt to cure the patient of mental or physical abnormalities. Later, a more sophisticated drill was invented that used a center spike to grip the skull for better control during the operation. This new improved instrument was called a "trephine." Trephining was also practiced by more 'scientific' physicians who offered the explanation that opening the skull provided some beneficial physical treatment for a patient's condition.

The ancient Greek philosophers, over two thousand years ago, developed a number of ideas about the brain and its relation to mind and behavior. For example, **Hippocrates** (c 460-370 B.C.), often called the first

doctor in Western Civilization, taught that illnesses come from the body, and often from the brain. He believed that the brain was the seat of intelligence and that diseases such as epilepsy arose from brain dysfunction. Hippocrates attempted to separate medicine from religion and superstition.

The philosopher **Plato** (c 428-348 B.C.) believed the brain was the seat of the mind, though his student **Aristotle** (384-322 B.C.) brought back the earlier belief that emotions and thoughts arose from the heart. For Aristotle, the brain was but a cooling tower for the blood. To some extent the idea of the mind and emotions emanating from the heart is still with us today. We don't say, "Memorize it by brain," and we don't give our loved ones a picture of our brain on Valentine's Day!

The chief doctor of the Roman Empire, **Galen** (129-199 A.D.), dissected brains of animals and concluded that the **cerebellum** controlled muscle movements and the **cerebrum** processed the senses. Pretty good, for a scientist working nearly two thousand years ago and for whom dissecting human cadavers was forbidden! Galen also hypothesized that animal spirits passed through the ventricles to carry messages through the brain to the body.

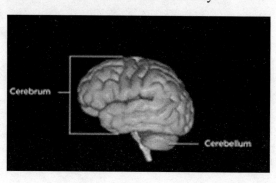

The understanding of electrical and chemical transmission through the nervous system was still far off, as was the idea that *cells* in the brain were doing the job.

Some of the earliest ideas linking the mind to illness date to about one thousand years ago. A Persian physician named **Avicenna** (c 980-1037) wrote in *The Canon of Medicine* that heart rate, somatic illnesses, depression, and other mental disorders were associated with emotions. This was likely the first excursion into what we now know as **physiological psychology** – study of the connection between minds and bodies.

Modern Brains

The first modern philosopher was a Frenchman named **René Descartes** who lived from 1596 to 1650. Descartes was a genius in mathematics, and in fact he invented analytical geometry (the graphs that we make are named after him – using his name in Latin they are known as Cartesian planes). Descartes is known for his **rational** approach to philosophy. That is, he wanted to discover the truths about the world through logical reasoning. Descartes decided to reject everything he had been taught and to construct his ideas of truth through careful, logical reasoning. He began with a simple idea that has become very well known and important. The first, most basic truth that Descartes recognized as undeniably true was the now well-known maxim: **I think, therefore I am** (in Latin: **Cogito, ergo sum**). Descartes believed that since he was able to experience his own thoughts, memories, and awareness of the world, he must therefore exist.

Descartes separated the mind from the body and declared that they were two different kinds of things. Descartes argued that our bodies are made of physical substances – molecules, atoms, and so on – and as such were subject to the physical laws of the universe and could legitimately be studied. On the other hand, the mind, he argued, was not a physical thing, it was like a ghost or a spirit, and therefore was not subject to physical laws. The mind was free, Descartes said, completely separate from the physical world. This viewpoint is known as **dualism**. Most brain scientists and philosophers today do not accept dualism as well-reasoned. Neuroscientists argue that mental phenomena emanate from the physical brain, and are therefore physical products that do follow physical laws. This view is known as **monism** (one kind of thing).

Descartes had reasoned that our brains control the movements of our bodies, but that our brains receive their instructions from our minds. Other thinkers disagreed, arguing that there is no way that a nonphysical thing could make a physical thing move. Descartes believed that our minds interact with our brains via a small gland, the **pineal gland**, located about in the middle of the brain. For Descartes, the pineal gland was where the mind and soul connected with the brain. Dualists say the mind controls the brain, while monists claim the brain controls the mind. Philosophers still argue about this issue, although brain scientists are firmly in the monist camp.

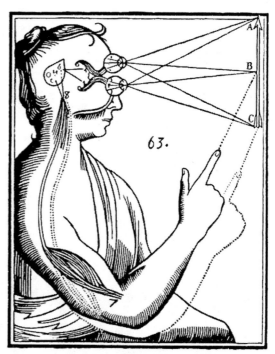

A drawing made by Descartes showing light entering the eyes and the message sent to the pineal gland.

Finding Functions

Franz Joseph Gall (1758-1828) was the first major proponent of the idea of "localization of function" in the brain. About two hundred years ago most neurologists believed that the brain worked as a whole, as an integrated organ, like the liver or kidneys. Some, however, like Gall, thought that different areas of the brain had different functions regulating specific parts of the body, personality characteristics, or mental abilities. Unfortunately, the specific jobs attributed to different areas of the brain were not determined by scientific research, but rather by casual observation and intuition. For example, Gall noticed that two people he knew both had protruding foreheads and also good memories; therefore he concluded that the front region of the brain (since it bulged out in those two people) must be the seat of memory.

Gall reasoned that certain parts of the brain are associated with certain traits or abilities. He labeled the brain functions using common, unambiguous terms that were

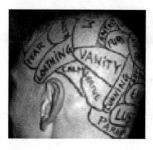

familiar in English usage and that fit the conceptual ideas of his time regarding human personality and mental qualities – such terms as hope, self-esteem, benevolence, parental love, friendship, acquisitiveness, conjugality, sublimity, spirituality, veneration, mirthfulness, ideality, murder, cautiousness, and similar common terms to label areas of the brain. Forty-two functions were assumed by Gall and were supposedly located in the brain where the head bulged out. The result was that a

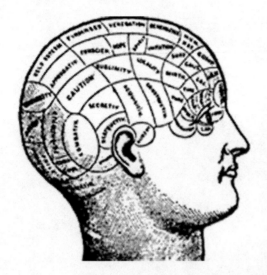

person's personality and intellect could be "read" by feeling or measuring the bumps and grooves on his head! This approach became known as **phrenology** and it experienced not only a wide popular following, similar to astrology, but also was adopted by medical doctors who would feel the bumps on a patient's head while attempting to make a diagnosis.

Gall had a great many believers who helped make phrenology a popular and money-making enterprise. Phrenology went beyond a pseudo-scientific theory and became both a cult and a profitable business. In fact, in 1907, the **Lavery electric phrenometer** was introduced, which consisted of an elaborate half-sphere metal frame that when placed on a person's head would measure the skull's bumps with "scientific precision." Of course, this

was nonsense. The electric phrenometer is now an instrument of historical interest and human curiosity and can be seen at The Museum of Questionable Medical Devices in Minneapolis, Minnesota or the Psychology Archives at the University of Akron. There you can sit under the metal helmet while an electric printer scrolls out your personality profile.

The Holistic Brain

Phrenology received its greatest criticism from the nineteenth century's most influential brain researcher, **Pierre Flourens** (1794-1867). Flourens was aghast at the wild conjectures being made by phrenologists and believed that the correct methodology for knowing the brain was careful experimentation. His means of investigation was the method of ablation, commonly used in brain research in the past. Certain sections of an animal's brain were ablated (surgically destroyed) and then the behavioral consequences were observed. Gall referred to such ablation techniques as "mutilation," and the experimenters as "mutilators."

At any rate, Flourens brought a high degree of precision to ablation, much more than was previously done, and he always carefully nursed his animals back to health after the surgery. Through such skillful and meticulous work, Flourens was able to uncover the basic functions of the cerebellum and cerebral lobes. Based on this carefully done research, Flourens and the rest of the medical establishment ultimately rejected the idea that

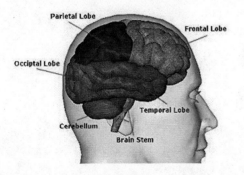

specific, precise faculties could be located in tiny, isolated areas of the brain. Instead, Flourens concluded from his research (no doubt partially because of his contempt for phrenology) that the brain is a holistic and integrated system.

For a time, brain researchers virtually abandoned their interest in finding specific functional areas of the brain. Instead researchers adopted the idea that the brain worked as a whole functioning organ. Although Gall and Flourens vehemently disagreed about localization of function in the brain, there can be no question that they and other researchers were in unequivocal agreement about one thing: The brain is the locus of the mind.

Rod in the Head

The well-known case of **Phineas Gage** (1823-1860), a Vermont railroad worker who in 1848 survived an explosion which propelled a metal spike up through his cheekbone and out the top of his head, was one of the first and most complete case histories detailing the characteristic mental changes associated with brain injury and, most telling, the public's surprised response to such a connection. Gage was distracted while tamping down some explosive powder with a long iron rod. He accidentally struck a rock with his rod, which emitted a spark that ignited the powder, thus causing an explosion. The iron rod, over three feet long, was later found fifty yards away with bits of blood and brain on it. It had passed straight through Gage's head, entering below the left eye and exiting through the top of his skull. The metal spike has since been donated to the Museum of the Harvard University Medical School where it is displayed with an inscription saying something like, "This is the rod that passed through the head of Phineas Gage."

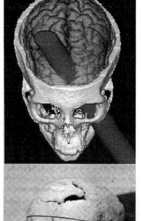

Although Gage recovered physically from the trauma, his friends and his doctor said he just wasn't the same Phineas anymore! We now know that the mental and behavioral changes experienced by Phineas Gage are representative of people who suffer damage to the brain's frontal lobe. These changes include the compulsive desire to collect and hoard things. In fact, Phineas Gage carried the metal rod with him obsessively for many years after his accident.

Gage's accidental injury caused major changes in his mental life. The changes were documented by his doctor, John Harlow, who wrote, "The equilibrium, or balance so to speak, between his intellectual faculties and animal propensities seems to have been destroyed. He is fitful, irreverent, indulging at times in the grossest profanity, which was not previously his custom, manifesting but little deference for his fellows, impatient of restraint or advice when it conflicts with his desires, at times pertinaciously obstinate, yet capricious and vacillating, devising many plans of future operation which are no sooner arranged than they are abandoned in turn for others appearing more feasible."

Today we would not find it strange that severe frontal lobe damage to the brain would cause significant changes to personality, emotions, language, and behavior. But at that time, one hundred and some years ago, the public did not understand the connection between the brain and psychological characteristics, so Gage's case was quite an eye-opener (pun intended!).

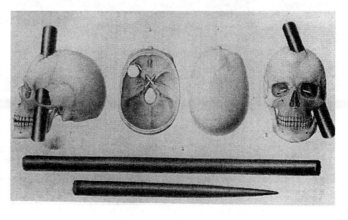

Modern brain researchers Antonio Damasio and his wife Hanna have resurrected the case of Phineas Gage. Using a computer model and photographs of Gage's skull (which also was saved by Harvard Medical School), they have determined the exact brain damage that Gage suffered and have studied patients with similar injuries. Their work can be found in *Descartes' Error* (1994).

Electrical Stimulation

In a scene reminiscent of a low-budget horror movie, German anatomist **Gustav Fritsch** (1837-1927) and psychiatrist **Eduard Hitzig** (1839-1907), working in the kitchen of Fritsch's home, surgically exposed the brain of a living dog (without the use of an anesthetic!), and using a thin needle electrode, applied an electrical current to various sections of the dog's exposed cortex! The year was 1870. Other early researchers had experimented with the application of various chemical substances, such as sodium chloride, wax, and corrosive substances, to the brains of unanesthetized animals, the result almost always being a severe, sometimes lethal, loss or impairment of functions in the poor animals. In one such case, in a series of experiments reported in 1871, a heated mixture of wax and tallow was injected into the area between the skull and the brain in dogs. Fritsch

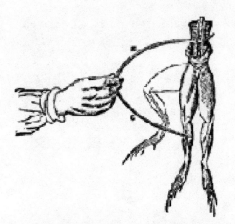

and Hitzig did not use chemicals in their research, but were among the first scientists to use electrical stimulation of a living brain.

Hitzig himself had previously applied battery wires to the brains of soldiers whose skulls had been opened by gunshots, giving him a rather deservedly ghoulish reputation. While a physician in the German Army, he had applied electric current to the exposed brains of soldiers and discovered that stimulation of different brain areas resulted in the movement of various muscles of the body. He got this idea from the discovery by **Luigi Galvani** (1737-1798) that a frog's muscle would contract when excited with electricity. Hitzig teamed up with Fritsch to see what would happen when the brain was so stimulated. Through their crude experiments on animals, working on a dressing table, Fritsch and Hitzig identified what is today called the "motor area" of the brain, which controls the muscles of the body. Their main work was published in a classic work of neuroscience titled *About the Electrical Excitability of the Brain.*

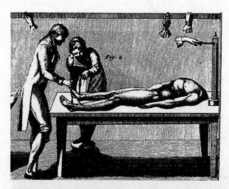

In 1802 **Giovanni Aldini** (1762-1834) performed bizarre experiments in which he applied electric current to the bodies of recently hanged and sometimes decapitated prisoners, using the same methods that his uncle Luigi Galvani had employed to stimulate nerves and muscles of animals. To gasps of horror by the populace, Aldini demonstrated how electrical stimulation evoked responses such as blinking and opening the eyes, facial grimaces, and tongue, eye and limb movements. He was not stimulating the brain, however; Aldini was causing movements in the dead bodies by stimulating the muscles directly. Incidentally, Mary Shelley's idea for *Frankenstein* (1818) likely came from her fascination with Aldini's exhibitions.

David Ferrier (1843-1928), a Scottish neurologist working in Yorkshire and later in London, performed a series of animal experiments intended to map the functions of the cortex. He used direct electrical stimulation of the brains of animals. His results were reported in the influential book *The Functions of the Brain*, published in 1876. His subjects were dogs, cats, rabbits, pigeons, frogs, fish, and other animals. One of the beneficial outcomes of his research was the use of his maps of the monkey brain to guide the first surgical operation locating and removing a brain tumor in a human patient.

Ferrier was able to identify brain areas for: a) vision, in the back of the brain, in the occipital lobe; b) hearing, at the side of the cortex, in the temporal lobe; and c) touch, the so-called "somatosensory area," just behind the motor strip, at the top of the cortex, in the parietal lobe. The experiments with electrical stimulation of the brain were achieving fantastic results and were remarkably influential.

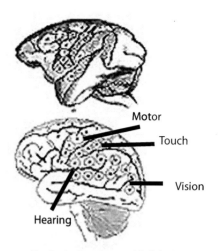

Ferrier's drawings with labels added.

Electrical Mapping of the Brain

In the mid-twentieth century, neurosurgeon **Wilder Penfield** (1891-1976), who founded the internationally known Montreal Neurological Institute in 1935, conducted research on epileptic patients. While at Oxford, Penfield had been influenced by world-famous neurologist **Charles Sherrington** (1857-1952) and decided then that he wanted to do brain research. One of the first brain operations he performed in Montreal was on his sister Ruth, who unfortunately later died of brain cancer in spite of the temporary respite she enjoyed after Penfield's aggressive removal of her diseased brain tissue.

Dr. Wilder Penfield, who mapped the cortex by electrical stimulation.

Students of neurology around the world were fascinated and enthralled by the Penfield team's research efforts and successes. Using direct electrical stimulation of the brain, Penfield's goal was to find the neurological locus of the auras that his epileptic patients experienced, and then remove the diseased brain tissue.

Starting in 1928, over 400 such operations were performed by Penfield's team. Volunteer patients whose epilepsy was unresponsive to medication were given a local anesthetic so they would be conscious during the operation. The surgeon opened the skull and using a "gentle electrical current" probed the cortex for the source of the aura, placing small numbers on the cortex. The malfunctioning section of the brain was then surgically removed, typically with significant improvement in the patient's condition.

But the success of this new treatment for epilepsy was not what amazed the world. The most astonishing finding was that Penfield's electrical stimulations were uncovering what appeared to be very precise localized areas in the brain for such human faculties as memories, visions, emotions, feelings, dreams, illusions, hallucinations, music, flashbacks, and other similar mental experiences. When their brains were electrically stimulated, these patients often reported conscious experiences of a very specific nature. A probe at the brain region Penfield had labeled number 8 and the patient heard her father's voice. When area number 11 was stimulated, the patient heard a violin playing in the room. Number 14 evoked the smell of onion, number 3 a tingling in the right index finger, number 6 a memory of childhood, and so on.

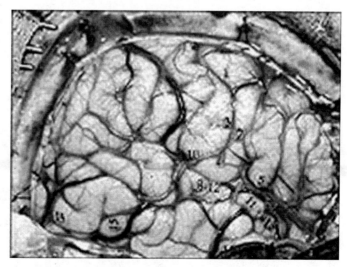

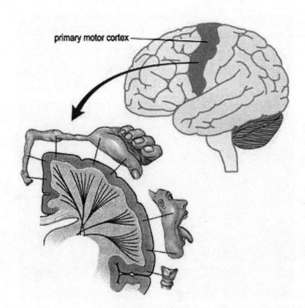

primary motor cortex

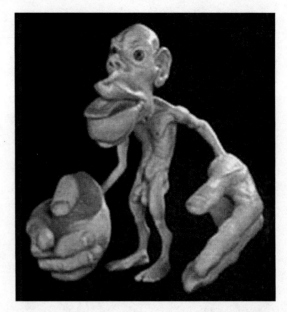

Electrical probing of the cortex revealed much more localization than had previously been assumed, and for a wider variety and for different, much more specific responses than anyone had anticipated. Penfield reported his findings in a 1937 paper that also provided detailed **homunculi** of brain areas for body movement and feeling, and again in the classic book, *The Cerebral Cortex of Man: A Clinical Study of Localization of Function* (1950), which he co-authored with Theodore Rasmussen.

These representations of brain areas are still widely used in psychology textbooks, although new research has found much more overlap between areas than Penfield noted. This overlap is because brain cells work in teams rather than in a one-to-one match with body parts, and also because the cells are adaptive and can change functions by joining other teams. Penfield later summarized his results in *Speech and Brain Mechanisms* (1959). His daring and provocative research opened the door for electrical exploration of other, even more exotic brain functions.

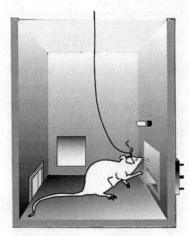

Olds and Milner in 1954 discovered a "**pleasure center**" in a rat's brain by placing an electrode into a particular area of the hypothalamus. When the rat pushed a lever the electrode delivered a small electric stimulation. The researchers were stunned to find that the rat pushed the lever nearly non-stop, forgoing all other incentives, including food and sex. A similar "pleasure center" has been located in the hypothalamus of the human brain.

Even more flabbergasting, **Jose Delgado**, professor of physiology at Yale University, used remote-controlled electrical stimulation of the brain to control the behavior of animals in the 1960s and 1970s. The research was startling, and a bit macabre – in one case Delgado went into a ring with a charging bull, but when he pushed the button on his "stimoceiver," the raging bull abruptly pulled up. Delgado made outrageous claims about the future of mind control using electric stimulation to the brain such as, "We must electronically control the brain. Someday armies and generals will be controlled by electric stimulation of the brain." Delgado's results were provocative enough to inspire grand ethical debates. Similar debates continue today in the field of neuroethics.

In the 1960s, Jose Delgado stopped a charging bull using remote control electrical stimulation of a region in the bull's brain.

Visualizing Brain Cells

In 1873, the Italian scientist **Camillo Golgi** (1843-1926) was working in a psychiatric hospital and discovered a staining technique that allowed him to see entire brain cells in exquisite detail. This technique was then known as the "black reaction," but is now called the **Golgi stain**.

The technique allowed the scientist **Santiago Ramón y Cajal** (1852-1934) to make beautiful, detailed drawings of neurons, which he called "butterflies of the soul," based on his theory that neurons were the mechanism by which mental states were produced. Golgi and Ramón y Cajal were scientific rivals and had different ideas about neurons (Ramón y Cajal proved to be right: Neurons are the mechanism by which the brain processes information). The two scientists shared the Nobel Prize in Physiology or Medicine in 1906, and for perhaps the first time the two great rivals shook hands and shared a word or two.

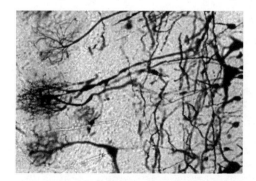

Golgi stain (on left), Santiago Ramón y Cajal at his desk, and one of his drawings of neurons.

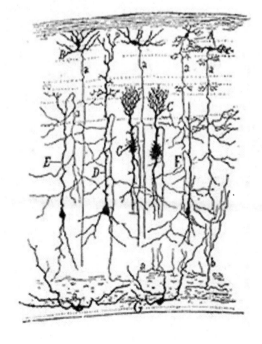

Measuring the speed of a neuron was the next great step forward for brain science. **Hermann von Helmholtz** (1821-1894) was a prolific German scientist who made important contributions to philosophy, psychology, and physics. His research and theories about vision and hearing were inspiring and are even useful today. Helmholtz devised a method of measuring the speed of a signal through the body's nerves and noted that it was immensely slower than electricity. This meant that the nerves in the body were not conducting electricity, but were using a biological process involving electrical potentials; neurons used a biological mechanism to send signals through the brain and the body. The mind was perhaps the result of biological events. This was an inspiring insight.

One of Helmholtz's students, **Wilhelm Wundt**, (1832-1920) went on to establish the first laboratory for the scientific study of the mind in Leipzig, Germany in 1879. This is widely considered to be the beginning of scientific psychology. The first American psychologist, **William James** (1842-1910), wrote in the first psychology textbook: "…a certain amount of brain-physiology must be presupposed or included in Psychology" (1890).

Early researchers realized that neurons responded both to electricity and to chemicals. It took many years to delineate the exact biological mechanisms that allow signals to travel through our bodies and brains. As Helmholtz theorized, it is not electricity that travels, but a biological process. That process allows electrical potentials to be created within brain cells by the movement of electrically charged particles (ions) in and out of the membranes of the neurons. This ion movement occurs through tiny openings called ion channels. The Nobel Prize in Chemistry in 2003 was awarded to scientists who discovered a technique for imaging and measuring the structure of an ion channel.

Above, Wundt, the first experimental psychologist, in his lab. Right, the first American psychologist, William James. Below, illustration of a synapse in which chemicals pass from one neuron to another. Top of next page, Loewi's experiment showed that chemicals influence nerve conduction.

Neurons communicate with each other at a place called a **synapse**. The term was coined by neurologist Charles Sherrington and his colleagues in 1897, and literally means "to clasp together." However, though physiologists knew about the synapse, they did not know how it worked. **Otto Loewi** (1873-1961), called the father of neuroscience, performed the critical experiment in 1921 proving that synapses were a chemical process of communication. **Henry Dale** (1975-1968) then isolated the first transmitter substance, **acetylcholine**.

Today there are known to be hundreds of **neurotransmitters** that send a signal at the synapse. In 1954 it became possible to see the synapse using an

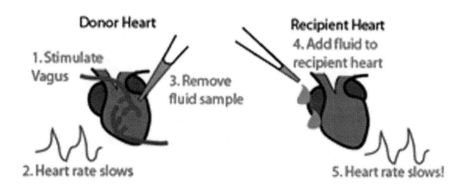

electron microscope, and the creation of microelectrodes makes it possible today to study the electrophysiology of synapses with precision. Microelectrodes also make it possible today for researchers to record the firings of single neurons in a living brain.

Return to Localization

The French physician **Paul Broca** (1824-1880) was collecting the brains of his patients who had died and had given him permission to examine them at autopsy. He noticed that damage to a specific region of the frontal lobe was associated with language impairment. This confirmed the idea of localization of function, and also advanced the idea that the mind is a phenomenon that is derived from brain functions.

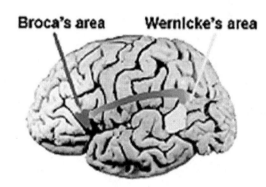

The area of the brain that Broca described is now known as **Broca's area**. Subsequently, a German scientist, **Carl Wernicke** (1848-1905), discovered another language area in the temporal lobe of the brain, now known as **Wernicke's area**. Localization was making grand headway (pun intended!).

What was needed next was a map of the brain that allowed scientists to use the same nomenclature to refer to specific brain locations. German scientist **Korbinian Brodmann** (1868-1918) undertook this task and created a brain map that contained fifty-two distinct regions, which he numbered. The result is a geographical depiction of a numbered brain known as **Brodmann areas**. Researchers could then refer to a specific brain region by a particular Brodmann number. Many of the Brodmann areas have subsequently been linked to psychological and biological functions; for instance, areas 1, 2, 3 are the somatosensory cortex, and area 4 is the motor strip.

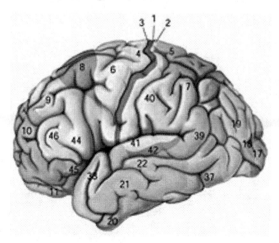

As brain scientists were learning more about the functions of specific areas of the brain, surgeons were seeking treatments that took advantage of such knowledge. Operating on the brain in an attempt to change psychological functioning is known as **psychosurgery**. The first common psychosurgery was the **lobotomy**, performed from the 1930s to 1950s, and even a few as late as the 1980s. The lobotomy was one of many invasive treatments developed in the early 20th century, including **electroconvulsive therapy** (ECT), which involves delivering electric current to the head to produce a seizure while the patient is unconscious. In fact, ECT is still an effective treatment for mood disorders today. Psychiatric drugs were not introduced until the 1950s.

A lobotomy was a surgical procedure that severed brain cells in the prefrontal lobe; hence the term "prefrontal lobotomy." Patients often became very subdued afterward. Oddly, these brain operations were deemed a great success and thousands of them were performed. In fact, **Egas Moniz** (1874-1955), the Portuguese physician who introduced the procedure in 1936, won the Nobel Prize in Physiology or Medicine. Some patients did quite well after a lobotomy, which shows the resilience of the brain, while others were worsened, and still others died from the procedure.

American psychiatrist **Walter Freeman** traveled around the United States performing a type of lobotomy he championed, called a transorbital lobotomy, in which he stuck an ice pick device through a person's eye sockets above the eyeballs, and pounded it with a hammer breaking through the thin bone behind the eyes, and then swished the ice pick back and forth, thereby destroying a chunk of the frontal lobe. Freeman promoted the ice pick lobotomy as a cure for many mental illnesses, and even performed a lobotomy on a daughter of Joseph Kennedy (father of John, Ted, and Bobby). Rosemary Kennedy was

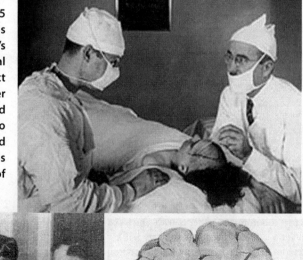

The prefrontal lobotomy was first performed in 1935 and continued until even the 1980s. On the right is shown a lobotomy requiring opening the patient's skull. Below, Walter Freeman developed transorbital lobotomy in which he pounded an ice pick-like object into the patient's eye sockets and into the brain in order to destroy parts of the frontal lobe. A lobotomized brain is shown in which you can see the damage to the frontal lobes (arrows). Dr. Freeman performed lobotomies on thousands of patients before losing his license. Some of his patients improved, but some of them died.

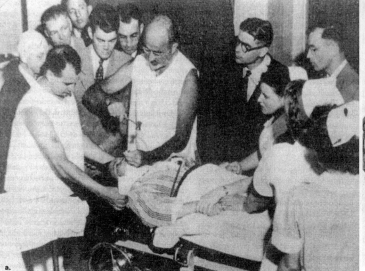

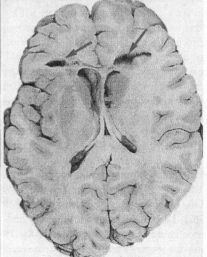

worsened by the operation and she subsequently spent her life in an institution. Freeman performed over 4,000 lobotomies before his medical license was revoked. Eventually it became clear that simply quieting patients was not necessarily a cure for psychological disorders, and anyway, medications and other treatments were gaining favor, so lobotomies gradually faded away; today psychosurgery is more rare and more precise.

In the 1950s and beyond, localization of function was advanced enormously because of research by Canadian psychologist **Brenda Milner** on a patient known as **H.M.** (Henry Molaison), who had his hippocampi removed surgically to save his life from severe epilepsy. The result of the removal of his temporal lobes was that H.M. could not form any new declarative (conscious) memories. Because of this amazing finding, H.M. became perhaps the most studied person in the history of psychology, with research discoveries that re-shaped our understanding of different types of memories and the learning process as it occurs in the brain. Shortly after his death in 2008, H.M.'s brain was sliced into histological sections live on the Internet while watched by thousands of scientists.

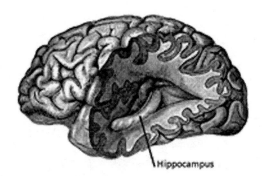

Today and Tomorrow

A confluence of disciplines as varied as philosophy and neurology is today forming a new science of the mind that promises a major alteration, a revolution, in our understanding of behavior, emotions, and mental phenomena. Emerging from this effort is a conception of the mind that is so foreign to common notions, so at odds with the views of the average person, so challenging and fantastic, that this idea is called *The Astonishing Hypothesis* (1994) by **Francis Crick**, Nobel laureate co-discoverer of the DNA double helix. Crick is at the forefront of mind science and has adamantly urged other scientists to dive into the study of human consciousness. Earlier, famed American scientist **Carl Sagan** (1934-1996) expressed the same astonishing notion: "My fundamental premise about the brain is that its workings – what we sometimes call 'mind' – are a consequence of its anatomy and physiology and nothing more." And, contemporary neurologist **Oliver Sacks** has written many books detailing the sometimes incredible changes that occur in a person when specific brain areas are damaged, such as *The Man Who Mistook His Wife for a Hat* (1985), and has written about people Sacks calls "differently brained," as in *An Anthropologist on Mars* (1995) and *The Mind's Eye* (2010).

Research and theory from myriad fields are converging and uniting to provide an astonishing picture of the mind as a physical component of the natural world, subject to scientific laws, accessible to experimentation, and therefore open to understanding, prediction, and control. The mind, it turns out, is not the elusive, fuzzy, non-corporeal entity as imagined for thousands of years. This new perspective unveils a mind that is purely and exclusively an emergent property of brain activity and thus can be analyzed, scrutinized, and revealed using contemporary research, technical procedures, and scientific models. The implications of this revelation are still unclear, but are inexorably unfolding and, undoubtedly, will engender both hopes and fears.

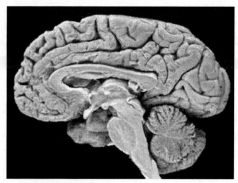

Brain Sciences

The discipline of scientific psychology is concerned with studying the ABCs: Affect (emotions, moods, and temperaments), Behavior (actions inside the body, as well as in the environment), and Cognition (perception, memory, thinking, and reasoning). The fascinatng thing is that all of these – all of the ABCs – are produced by the brain. That is why scientific psychologists are now paying such a great deal of attention to the organ in our heads. After all, the brain is the locus of the mind and the controller of behavior. It is where psychological experiences are formed and memories are created and stored. It is where "it" is at.

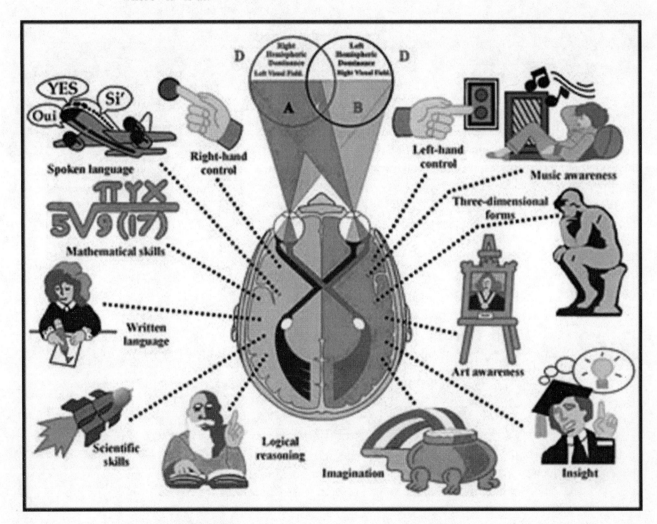

Roger Sperry (1913-1994) won the Nobel Prize for his research on people who had their cerebral hemispheres separated in a special surgical procedure to save their lives. Through his research, Sperry was able to discover many of the different functions of the left and right sides of the human cerebrum. **Michael Gazzaniga** was Sperry's student and now continues this line of research. Gazzaniga has been studying split-brain patients for over three decades.

One day in the 1970s, Gazzaniga got into a taxi cab in New York City with a cognitive psychologist named George Miller, who was famous for his paper about the capacity of short-term memory: "The Magic Number 7 plus or minus 2." While in the cab,

Gazzaniga and Miller decided that a name was needed for the new branch of psychology that studies how the brain is related to various cognitive properties. They coined the term, **cognitive neuroscience**. Today this field is a huge endeavor that includes scientists from many different disciplines such as evolutionary psychology, anthropology, linguistics, philosophy, bioethics, and artificial intelligence.

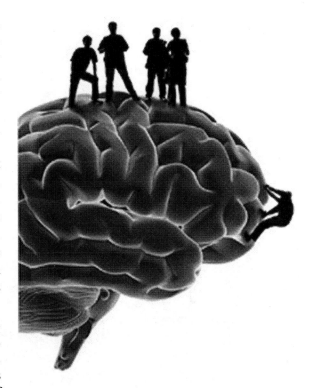

There are many different disciplines that attempt to understand the brain and its role in our mental life, our actions, thoughts, memories, and experiences. **Neuroscience** is a branch of biology that studies the parts and processes of the nervous system, particularly the brain. There are many subfields of neuroscience that specialize in smaller topics. The field that studies the process of brain development within an individual, from womb to tomb, is called **developmental neuroscience**, for example.

Biological psychology, or **biopsychology**, attempts to relate all components of animal biology, such as hormones, cell biology, heredity, and the brain, to psychological properties. **Behavioral neuroscience** is very similar to biopsychology, but emphasizes aspects of behavior and their neural substrates (the parts and processes of the brain that contribute to, create, or influence behaviors). There are even sub-divisions of psychology today called **social neuroscience** and **cultural neuroscience**, which are interested in how brain processes are related to social interaction and cultural differences between peoples. For example, one study reported differences between people from East Asian and Western cultures in brain activity in the visual areas associated with perceptual processing (Park & Huang, 2010).

And, of course, one of the most fascinating and most active of these many subfields of psychology is cognitive neuroscience. This approach often uses ideas from **cognitive psychology**, the sub-area of psychology that studies the mind and its components, including topics such as attention, problem solving, perception, and memory. Cognitive neuroscience attempts to find the neural substrates for these various cognitive functions.

Perhaps we need a term that encompasses all of these sub-disciplines of psychology and biology, these specialized fields that attempt to link brain and nervous system to psychological processes of mind, emotion, and behavior. Let us use the term **psychological neuroscience** as an umbrella expression for the sciences that investigate how the brain subserves affect, behavior, and cognition – the domains of scientific psychology.

Research in the brain sciences exists today at an impressive level that fascinates us all. No doubt the results of future research in psychological neuroscience will continue to inspire, inform, amaze, and surprise us for many decades to come.

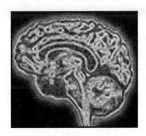

Chapter 3

BRAIN DEVELOPMENT
How do you make a brain?

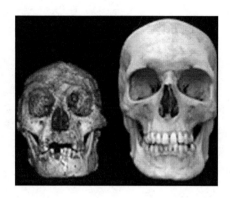

$\mathcal{T}\!he\ term\ ``evolution"$ refers to changes in the genetics and
inherited traits of a species or population that occur in successive generations over very
long periods of time. The term "**development**," on the other hand, refers to changes in an
individual over his or her life-span. A species evolves, while a person develops.

Evolution occurs because of changes in the genetic material that pass to offspring.
These changes will continue in the genome if they help reproduction. This process is
called **natural selection**. When the environment changes, any traits that
help survival, and hence reproduction (being passed on to offspring), will
continue in the genome. Traits that do not help reproduction will gradually
fade out.

Brains, of course, went through a long history of evolution and
natural selection. Human brains evolved the ability to learn and remember,
to use language, to be intelligent, and to think abstractly. Development, on
the other hand, is about how an individual changes over time. Our brains
develop from womb onward. Development depends not only on genetic
factors, but on our experiences in the world. Before giving details about brain
development, it would first be useful to think a bit about brain evolution.

Evolving Brains

The very earliest animals on Earth, animals near the bottom of
the evolutionary tree, such as worms, snails, and insects, have very simple
brains that are, in essence, bundles of cells known as **ganglia**. A worm is the
simplest organism to have a central nervous system, though the brain of such
a lowly animal is not a command center because there are ganglia throughout

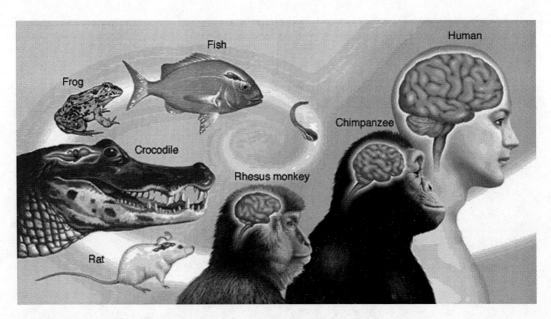

the body that have specific jobs. Even with its brain removed, a worm can perform many behaviors. What if we humans were like that? Insect's brains are miniscule, yet they can accomplish movement, sensing, mating, finding food, and other actions. So, it apparently does not take a humongous number of cells to control a variety of complicated behaviors.

A step or two up the evolution ladder gives us birds, reptiles, and fish, whose brains are small, but have some complex areas devoted to specific tasks. Smell and vision have separate modules in these brains, for instance. Though their brains are small, these animals have much more complex behaviors than worms or insects. Saying someone is a bird brain is not that much of an insult, really. We should probably use the term "worm brain" instead.

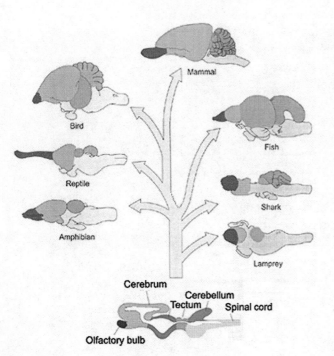

Mammals are another story, since they have evolved brains of various shapes and sizes. The largest brain is that of the blue whale, about four times the size of yours. However, size alone is not a perfect indicator of brain intelligence or computing ability. Whales don't do calculus. A bird's brain is much smaller than that of a whale, but they are both complex and efficient in their own way.

We might say that in general the larger the brain, the more intelligent the animal; but the ratio of brain to body is important, too, as well as how the brain is organized and which regions have evolved the most. Carnivores, for example, have larger brains than their prey, which perhaps is why they have an advantage – larger brains usually mean more complex behaviors.

Non-human animals at the highest levels of intelligence, such as chimpanzees and dolphins, have wrinkled brains just like us, compared to the smooth brains of less intelligent animals. A fetus's brain is smooth until about six months of development when the characteristic wrinkles begin to appear in the cerebrum.

A chimpanzee brain has lots of wrinkles, nearly similar to a human, but the front part of the brain is not as well evolved as in the human brain. Apparently, increase in the frontal lobe is the most recent change in the evolution of the human brain. Chimpanzees and humans separated in evolution many, many millions of years ago, reminding us that evolution is typically a very slow process.

Human brains evolved over a very long period of time, millions of years. Hominids of four million years ago had brains about one-fourth the size of present humans. **Homo erectus**, who lived nearly two million years ago, had bodies about the same size as present humans, yet their brains were half as large.

One of the most noticeable changes in human brain evolution is the massive size of the cerebrum, particularly in the front, relative to the lower brain areas, such as the brainstem. Other mammals have relatively large brainstems compared to us.

Also, the parietal lobe (top back part of brain) expanded and became more rounded in today's humans compared to our hominid ancestors, such as Neanderthal man. Perhaps the increase in the parietal lobe was associated with tool use and abstract, computational thinking. Contemporary anthropologists and evolutionary psychologists are interested in discovering the precise details of how natural selection gave rise to today's human brains that have such highly complex cognitive and language skills.

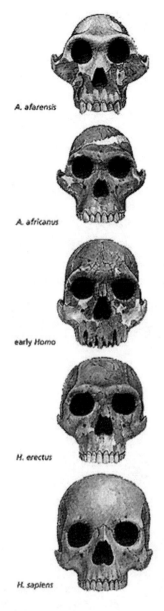

A. afarensis

A. africanus

early Homo

H. erectus

H. sapiens

Developing Brains

An adult human brain weighs about three pounds and contains about a hundred billion neurons (the brain cells that communicate). During the prenatal period, the brain develops more neurons than needed – in fact, the brain must develop neurons at a rate of about fifty thousand per second for most of the nine months in the womb. This large number of neurons is decreased just before and after birth. Still, at birth a baby has a huge number of neurons with a very dense structure of connections. (Thomas & Johnson, 2008).

The baby's brain has all possible connections and links ready to be consolidated into neural networks. Experience will determine which synapses become strong and which ones disappear. The baby will learn some things and not others (think about learning a specific

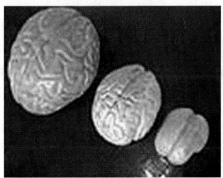

Adult, newborn, and premature brains.

language, for example – some synapses are strengthened and some vanish). By adolescence, the teenage brain has fewer neurons and synapses, but they are better organized into networks. Still, the teen brain has a ways to go to reach maturity.

The brain not only grows, it also develops intricately through a specific sequence of stages that are orchestrated by genetics. Many neurons are created in special regions and then move to their ultimate locations. During the period of the embryo, shortly after conception, the brain

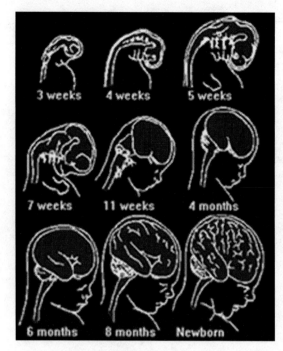

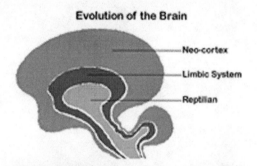

Evolution of the Brain

Neo-cortex

Limbic System

Reptilian

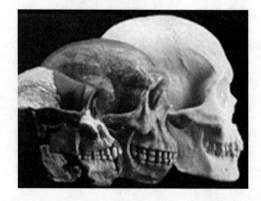

develops from a structure known as the **neural tube**. At the front of this structure cells proliferate and form the beginnings of a brain. Some of the cells will differentiate into neurons. These newly formed neurons develop from stem cells and migrate in the embryo to their positions in the brain. Neuronal migration is the process by which the developing neurons end up in their final destinations in the brain. These cells then grow dendrites and axons, the branches that grow out from the cell body and allow the neuron to receive and send signals. These newly formed neurons are like a tangle of unconnected electrical wires.

The branches of the neurons will continually reach out to each other and form chemical connections called **synapses**. A synapse is where one neuron communicates with another neuron. An arrangement of synaptic communications results in a **neural network**, much like computer software. As few as one hundred neurons can form a neural network that can control or modulate a specific behavior. Changes in the synapses occur during learning, and the resulting neural networks will support various motor and psychological functions such as movement of the body, memories, perceptions, thoughts, beliefs, behaviors, and our personalities.

Research in developmental neuroscience has found that neural networks are being created at an astonishingly high rate. There are periods, however, early in life when such networks are being formed the fastest and most efficiently, so called **critical periods** or **sensitive periods**. Brains are most plastic in the first years of life.

For example, the brain's visual cells organize by about four months of age. If not stimulated by that time, the baby will have impaired vision. Research found that if cats' eyes were covered at birth so that vision was blocked, the cats later would not develop normal vision (Trachtenberg, 2000). Also, cats raised in an environment in which they see only horizontal lines will not develop the brain cells that allow for perception of vertical lines (Held & Hein, 1963). A more recent study has added more precision to our understanding: Michael Crair and others (1998) found that the basic structure of the cat's visual cortex was innate, but experience was required for development of specific features of the cortical maps and for selectivity of neurons. So, a little bit of both heredity and experience helps organize the brain for perception.

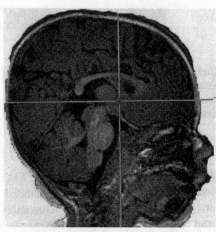

Brain of a 7-month old infant.

Another example is language. The critical period for language appears to be approximately up to six years old. A child who does not hear and imitate language by then will likely have language difficulties forever more. The parts of the brain that organize for understanding and expressing language are particularly sensitive to auditory and visual input during early childhood. If we try to learn a language later in life, the task is much more difficult. A language accent developed early in life is hard to change later.

Brains are not completely assembled and finished at the time of birth. Brains develop, and development is a process; we are not born with a fully formed brain. In addition, once the neural networks are established, they are still subject to possible changes. That is, brains are plastic, not static. They change with development and with experience. This ability to change, **plasticity**, is more pronounced in babies and children than later in life. However, research shows that even adult brains quickly reorganize with certain experiences. A musician who plays violin everyday will have larger brain regions (those for touch and movement of the hands) than before. If a person is blindfolded, then his or her brain will start to reorganize the normal visual processing region. Blind people, for example, use the visual part of the brain for perceiving touch. Brains change with experience, at least to some degree.

Teenage Brains

The human brain grows extremely fast during childhood and tapers off quickly after about three years of age. The brain of a two-year old is about four-fifths the size of an adult's. By six years old, the brain is 95% of its adult size. And, the cerebrum continues to get thicker throughout childhood as neural networks are being organized. The peak is reached around puberty. Then, more pruning occurs as the brain starts the process of maturation into adulthood – excess synapses are being discarded.

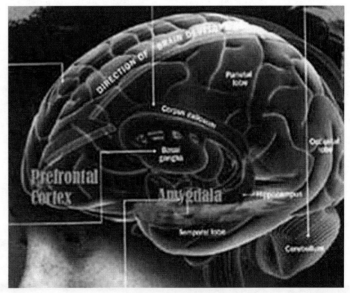

The teen-age brain is not the same as the mature, adult brain. We all recognize that teenagers are not the same as adults in their emotions, behaviors, and thinking. There are clear, significant differences between the brains of teens and adults. The brain's gray matter, the outer cortex of the cerebrum (the top, wrinkly part; the thinking part), continues to build up until about age 11 or 12, but then connections begin to thin out – a pruning process ensues. However, different brain regions mature at different times, and girls' and boys' brains show some differences in development; for example, girls' brains develop faster, with a proportionately larger frontal lobe, while boys' brains are larger on average, boys exhibit more disorders, such as attention difficulties, autism, intellectual delay, and speech problems.

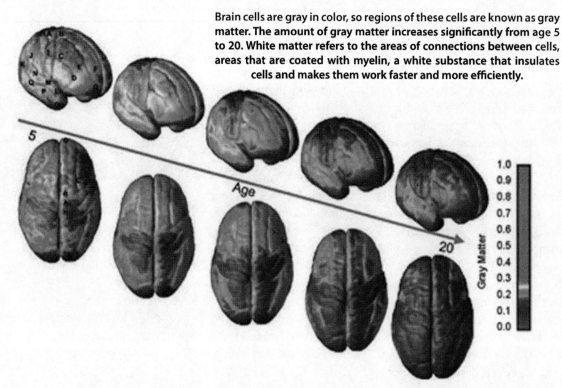

Brain cells are gray in color, so regions of these cells are known as gray matter. The amount of gray matter increases significantly from age 5 to 20. White matter refers to the areas of connections between cells, areas that are coated with myelin, a white substance that insulates cells and makes them work faster and more efficiently.

In general, areas of the brain related to sensing and movement mature earlier than areas for executive functions, such as decision-making and reasoning, areas that do not reach full potential until the early twenties. The brain's reward center is more active during adolescence than in adulthood, and connections between reasoning and emotions are lagging. The pruning that occurs at the beginning of adolescence is important because it likely means that connections that are used will survive, while those that are not used will disappear. So, for the teenager, maybe "use it or lose it" applies to brain development. The brain's white matter, the fatty myelin that coats and insulates brain cells making them work faster and more efficiently, continues its long-term development that soared in childhood, yet will not be completed until about the age of 24. The teen brain lags behind the young adult brain primarily in the frontal lobe.

So, the pattern that we see in the womb and early childhood of overproduction of brain cells and then pruning down as neural networks are organized occurs again as the child approaches adolescence. For teens, the frontal lobe is advancing, but the neural networks that give one the ability to plan, organize, and make careful decisions are not finished. This is when the brain is vulnerable to chemical assault, and, unfortunately, it is when teens begin experimenting with drugs and alcohol. Research confirms that teens who binge drink and use marijuana do worse on tests of cognitive ability, such as memory, spatial perception, and paying attention (Thoma, 2010).

In the adolescent years, the frontal lobe has not yet finished forming its connections with the lower, emotional brain, the limbic system, and particularly the amygdala. Therefore, the teenage brain is wired with a tendency to react emotionally and to not be especially proficient at controlling emotions by using the thinking frontal lobe. This is because the neural networks that bind thinking in the frontal lobe with emotions in the lower brain are not fully formed. For instance, when researchers showed teenagers a photo of a person exhibiting fear, the teenagers reacted emotionally to the photo, but could not rationally identify why they did so. Also, they were poor at identifying the emotion that was being expressed in the photo. Adults, on the other hand, identified it every time (Yurgelin-Todd, 2009).

The fact that the frontal lobe is not fully organized in adolescence suggests that teens would be more inclined toward risk-taking and impulsive behavior. Of course, we do not see this in all teens, but it is generally true; on average, an older adult tends to think a little longer than a teen does before responding to a situation, and is more likely to think about risks and to avoid them than is a teen. Perhaps, also, it means that teens are not as good at thinking about the consequences of an action; rather, they feel a strong emotion, have difficulty modulating it with the frontal lobe, and act on it before considering alternatives.

While teens may look physically mature, their cognitive ability to understand situations, weigh consequences, control emotions, and make rational decisions may lag behind. Adults may speak to physically mature teens assuming that their minds are mature too, and be in for a bit of a surprise. Teens seem to respond more with a gut reaction, more emotionally, more spontaneously, and less inhibited than do older adults.

Several changes are occurring in the teen brain. Here is a brief summary:

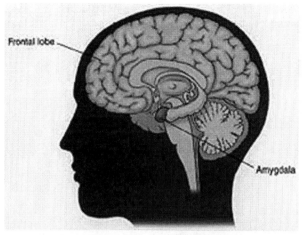

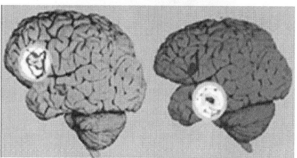

When looking at a face that is showing fear, an adult brain (left) shows more activation in the frontal lobe, while a teen brain (right) is more active in the amygdala.

1. The cerebellum, in the back below the cerebrum, is growing rapidly. This part of the brain coordinates movements, and likely helps coordinate thinking, too. Teens are beginning to develop coordination in their body movements, such as dancing and sports.

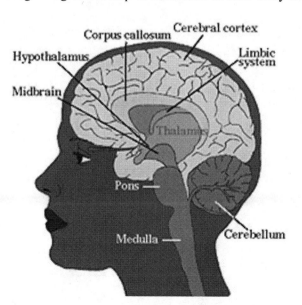

However, the cerebellum continues developing well into the 20s. Also, the cerebellum is influenced much more by experience than by heredity, so the teen years and early adulthood are excellent opportunities for developing coordinated muscle movements.

2. As mentioned above, the emotional part of the brain, the amygdala, takes precedence over the thinking cerebrum, so teens have quick, erratic emotions. The connections between the emotional brain and the thinking frontal lobe are not well developed, so teens are not good at modulating or recognizing emotional reactions.

Teens are more likely to have strong, changeable emotions that they can't explain or even recognize at times.

3. The frontal lobe of the cerebrum goes through a growth spurt around 11 or 12, then begins to prune back and organize. Teen years are a critical period for learning to think abstractly and for developing more complex reasoning skills. But, such development takes time and will not reach a peak for a decade or more, not until mid to late 20s.

4. The cable of nerves that connects the two hemispheres of the cerebrum, the **corpus callosum**, which is used for connecting thoughts and senses between the left and right sides of the brain, helping such cognitive skills as seeing the whole picture and creativity, also goes through a growth spurt during the teen years. Younger teens will not be as proficient at coordinating thoughts as are older teens and young adults.

The teen brain is a work in progress. Many cognitive abilities are not mature in adolescence, and it will take years for them to reach their peaks. During young adulthood – the college years and somewhat beyond – we see development of much calmer, less erratic emotions, more complex reasoning, less risk-taking, and better coordination of both body and thinking. But then, too soon, comes middle age, and a whole new set of issues.

The Aging Brain

It is normal to experience some cognitive loss in middle age, but there are fewer losses than popular rumors suggest. It's not all bad news, it's not all down hill, although, yes, aging brains show some decline. But, there are some improvements, too.

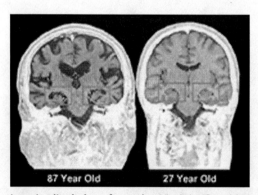

87 Year Old   27 Year Old

Longitudinal data from the Virginia Cognitive Aging Project found all mental abilities decline with age, but not as much as previously thought. Experts have called this a major public health problem, particularly as baby boomers age.

The major loss is in speed. A middle-aged or older brain is much slower at responding and processing than it was in young adulthood. Neurons are getting thinner, the cortex is getting thinner, and the result is a slowdown in the speed of neural signals – it takes longer to react, to learn, and to retrieve information.

The middle age brain makes more errors, experiences the tip-of-the-tongue phenomenon more often, and finds it more difficult to multi-task than did the young adult brain. Damage to brain cells begins to accumulate in middle age, which progresses even more rapidly in old age. Also, brain weight and volume decrease with age in older adulthood; for instance, at age 90 a brain will weigh about 5% to 10% less than it did at age 20. The grooves or wrinkles on the brain widen with aging, and the bumps on the surface get smaller. Structural changes in the temporal lobe, in an area important for word recognition, leave some older people with hearing loss. A common complaint of many in middle and old adulthood is difficulty recognizing words in a loud setting.

But, there is good news, too. In middle and older adulthood, brains show a number of somewhat surprising advancements over younger brains. Brains aren't getting any bigger as we move toward old age, but middle-aged and older brains can be getting better at complex reasoning, seeing the big picture, thinking holistically, recognizing patterns, making judgments, finding unique solutions to problems, and creating deeper understandings. We could say that cognitive expertise, at least in some avenues, reaches a peak in middle adulthood.

A funny thing happens to a woman's brain during pregnancy – it shrinks about 8%! This is probably the result of the bonding hormone **oxytocin** flooding the brain and restructuring circuits. The effect is temporary – brain size returns to normal about six months after giving birth. However, many women experience depression due to the hormonal changes, and some feel spacey due to sleep deprivation and stress, both major influences on brain functioning. As women move into menopause (average age of 51), hormone fluctuations also affect brain processes with resulting alterations in mood, energy, and attention.

An older brain may not think as fast as a younger brain, but it has advantages in other regards. However, to some extent this all depends on keeping the brain active and building pathways. Though slower, an older brain still is plastic and makes new connections. But, we should note that older brains respond differently to learning and to exposure to ideas than they did when they were young. Making new connections in the brain comes about through different experiences when we are older compared to a when we were teens. A younger brain typically builds new pathways through learning new material, while an older brain benefits greatly from experiences that challenge the assumptions and ideas that were learned when young. Older adults do better in brain development, for example, when they bump up against ideas that are different, maybe contrary, to their own.

Mid-life Concerns

Certainly, as people reach middle age and beyond, many begin to be concerned about losing their brain abilities such as memory, finding their way around, recognizing objects, and making judgments. There is a fear that brain cells will be lost and never recovered. But, research in this area offers some happy surprises: As long as people are healthy and free of brain disease they will maintain most of their brain cells for as long as they live. Also, brains continue to develop, change, and adapt well into old age.

There is more good news for middle-agers: The brain changes that occur in mid-life result in people being more satisfied and optimistic, not less. Moods become more stable, and even improve when the kids leave home. The **empty-nest syndrome** seems to be a myth for the majority. Similarly, the ability to care about others, to feel empathy, increases with age. It seems middle-aged brains are powering up, not powering down in some ways. Some cognitive skills that peak in mid-life include vocabulary, inductive reasoning, creativity, understanding the main point, and finding solutions to problems. There is no inevitability to **dementia** in old age. Most older people have intellectual abilities near or sometimes even better than when they were younger, though their cognition is slower.

Other than speed of processing, cognition generally improves during young adulthood, reaches a peak in middle age, and then levels off until late in life. IQ scores, for example, tend to be stable throughout most of early and middle adulthood, and only begin to drop, on average, after the age of 70 or 75. In fact, between ages 80 and 90, while many people will experience a slight drop in IQ score, many also will stay steady, and about 10% will see an increase in their scores. I hope you and I are both in that 10%!

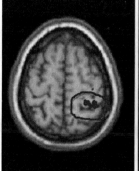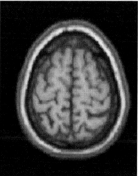

Brain scan shows older adult brain (left) is slower at processing than young adult brain (right) because of more cross-talk between hemispheres. The circle shows an area of increased activity in the old adult brain while engaged in the same task as the young adult brain.

It's true: Many older adults, and even many middle-aged adults, report some loss of memory. When it comes to memory, laboratory studies show a decrease in speed as we age, as well as a decrease in motivation. That is, older people get lower scores on experimental tests of memory partially because they don't care as much how well they do. Also, older adults who are taught memory techniques do nearly as well as younger adults.

Older adults who experience memory loss – and that does happen to lots of people as they age – are not losing brain cells, research shows, but rather their memory problems are due to chemical changes occurring in the aging brain; neurotransmitter chemicals are decreasing. For example, elderly brain cells produce less of the transmitter GABA. On the other hand, one study found that the visual cells of monkeys regained their youthful activity after being exposed to GABA (Leventhal, 2003).

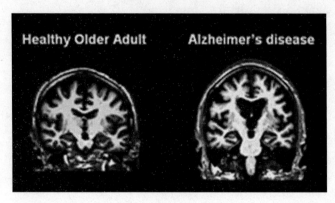

Now some cautionary news: All of the good news about the aging brain is dependent on the brain being disease free, free of large amounts of stress, and continuing to learn as it ages. Certainly, too many people as they approach and enter old age will suffer from brain dementia, such as Alzheimer's disease. About 5-8% of people over 65 have dementia. People under 65 sometimes develop dementia, but the incidence of dementia skyrockets in old age, doubling every five years after age 65.

Not only disease can slow a brain; middle-aged brains will decline, too, if they are not challenged. Stress is another factor that can slow brain development. Stress causes the release of hormones such as **cortisol** that can have a beneficial effect in the short-run, even helping memory, but in the long-run it causes damage to brain cells, particularly in the part of the brain sensitive to learning and memory. By the way, children raised in low socioeconomic environments have higher levels of cortisol and many more health problems (Chen, 2010). Long-term stress is not healthy.

In a sense, middle age is a fork in the road for brains. Research demonstrates that there are many experiences that will help the middle aged brain develop and fulfill its potentials. These include aerobic exercise, a proper diet (fruits, vegetables, antioxidants, low salt and red meat), adequate sleep, low body fat, low stress, and experiencing mental challenges.

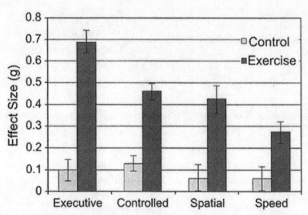

Adults over 60 who did aerobic exercise scored higher than a control group on four measures of cognitive ability (Colcombe, 2003).

While some experts say there is not yet enough evidence, many who study cognitive enhancement among middle aged and older adults have concluded that an intellectually stimulating environment helps stave off cognitive loss and dementia. However, training in specific areas, say solving puzzles, does not generalize to other cognitive tasks. But, training in executive functions, like planning, organizing, and working memory, will help keep minds sharp (Hertzog, 2008); the more complex and novel, the more the benefit. It is hypothesized that intellectual stimulation helps build brain circuitry and acts as a sort of "**cognitive reserve.**" Two people with the same amount of brain damage can have vastly different symptoms because one has built up more scaffolding in the brain.

In one typical case, Gary Small, director of the UCLA Center on Aging, had middle-agers work on a computer doing Google searches for an hour a day. After a week's worth of practice, their brains were scanned while doing a Google search. The results showed significant increases in the frontal lobe, the thinking part of the brain, and in areas that control memory and decision making. The researchers concluded that it appears that the experience altered neuron circuits, strengthening those for cognitive skills. Brains are plastic, apparently even into old age.

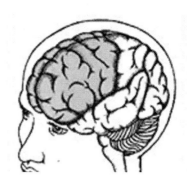

Imagine an Image

As the previous research example demonstrates, among the most common tools used by researchers of psychological neuroscience today are high-tech brain imaging machines. It is now possible to safely watch the brain of a person to discover which brain parts and brain physiology are active during behaviors, emotions, and cognitive functions such as reading, solving problems, thinking, reasoning, decision-making, and all other aspects of our mental lives.

These tools allow researchers to look at both the structure and various aspects of the functioning of a brain in a living person without invasion. Today, fortunately, we do not need to rely on brain research methods of the past, such as autopsy, electrical stimulation, surgery, or ablation (destruction of brain tissue), to examine a brain or to study the functions of specific brain regions. Today we can make a very clear image of a living human brain while it is performing any of its innumerable tasks in a living person lying in a high-tech chamber. Here are brief descriptions and explanations of some of the many brain imaging techniques that are now being used:

1. The Electroencephalogram (EEG)

Brains consist of cells that create electrical energy, and hence brains give rise to electrical signals that combine to form what are called **brain waves**. These electrical

patterns vary in intensity and frequency, qualities of electrical energy that can be measured by sensitive electrodes either placed directly on a person's scalp or embedded in an EEG cap that fits tightly on a person's head. A recording device then prints a picture of the oscillating, wavy electrical impulses that emanate from the brain onto a long, wide strip of paper, as well as projects them onto a computer screen. Although technically not a brain image, the EEG is an image of the rhythmic electrical firing of brain cells and can be attained without invasion in a living subject. Of course, the EEG can record abnormalities in a person's brain waves, such as those associated with epilepsy.

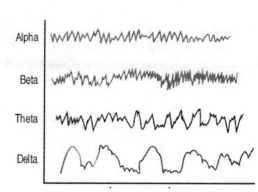

Brain waves are categorized according to their electrical characteristics. For example, **alpha waves** are regular, low-intensity waves associated with relaxation. In the 1960s it was common to see ads for machines that supposedly could help a person achieve an alpha wave state, a condition which purportedly would give the person a relaxed, meditative feeling. It's true that research on biofeedback has found that people can alter a number of their body

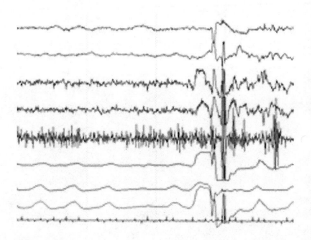

functions, including brain waves, if they have feedback information. Such **biofeedback** therapies have been helpful in many cases. However, machines sold through magazines such as *Reader's Digest* only measured facial twitches, so were a scam. But an EEG could be used to give accurate feedback to a person regarding their brain's production of alpha waves.

Another type of brain wave, **beta waves**, are active, irregular, low-intensity waves that indicate concentration and rapt attention. And still another type are **delta waves**, which are regular, high in amplitude, long in wavelength, and occur during deep sleep. When a person falls into a deep sleep, brain cells are firing in a kind of synchronized rhythm, therefore, delta wave sleep is sometimes called synchronous sleep (S-sleep) or **slow wave sleep** (SWS).

This deep stage of sleep when delta waves are common is also known as stage 4 **NREM** (pronounced "non-rem") sleep. On the other hand, during **REM** (rapid eye movement, pronounced "rem") sleep, brain waves are similar to those that occur when awake; thus the REM stage was originally called "paradoxical" sleep since the brain waves indicate awake, but the behavior indicates asleep.

NREM sleep, when the eyes are not moving around, is divided into four stages according to the brain wave patterns. These are simply called stages 1, 2, 3, and 4. When people fall asleep at night, typically they pass through these stages in order, deeper and deeper, before entering REM sleep, which occurs after maybe an hour and a half of sleeping. REM sleep is correlated with dreaming (dreaming is reported about 85% of the time when awakened during REM), and **theta waves** produced by the brain during REM sleep are believed to be the result of brain processes that are important for filtering information regarding the day's events (particularly emotion-producing experiences), and storing information into memory.

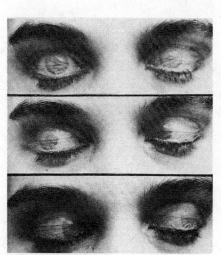

This time lapse photo shows the eye movements characteristic of REM sleep. The eyes apparently are following a dream. The rest of the body is paralyzed, presumably so the sleeper does not follow the dream with the rest of the body. That might be embarrassing!

As is obvious from the name, a person's eyes move about rapidly during REM; but the body proper is quite still, almost paralyzed, in a condition of **atonia**. Research has found that the moving eyes seem to be following the dream. Fortunately, the body does not act out the dream because the body is inhibited from moving during REM sleep by a switch in the brain that stops motor signals from getting to the body. Sleep walking and sleep talking therefore, do not typically occur during the REM stage, but are associated with the deeper stages of NREM sleep when brain waves are slow and synchronous. During REM, neurons are firing rapidly, individually, in an uncoordinated manner. Hence REM, or dreaming sleep, is sometimes referred to as **desynchronous** or **D-sleep**.

The EEG is the oldest noninvasive method of viewing brain activity. The first person to measure a brain's electrical patterns was German researcher Hans Berger in the 1920s. The EEG can be used to localize functions, but it is not a very accurate technology because the electrodes on the skull react more to surface electrical activity than to activity in deeper areas of the brain. However, the EEG may prove to be important in

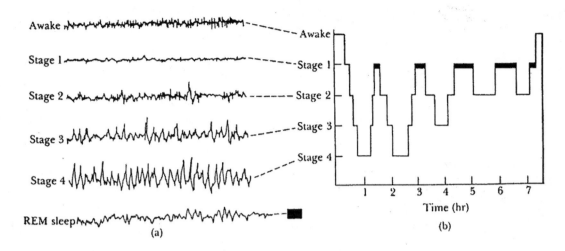

A sleep hypnogram shows (a) the stages of sleep as defined by brain waves, and (b) the amount of time spent in each stage during a sleep period.

contemporary research because many theorists are looking at the brain's electrical patterns as a possible solution to the binding problem – the question of how all the independent functions of the brain are pulled together into a coherent whole consciousness.

For example, Francis Crick and Christof Koch (1998) have hypothesized that consciousness may be dependent on signals from the thalamus that have a particular rate of oscillation. They have suggested a 40-Hertz rhythmic, coordinated firing of neurons. In a similar hypothesis, Rudolph Llinas (1998) has conjectured that a wave of neural impulses radiates from the thalamus to other brain regions in order to bind together and coordinate mental awareness in the here and now. Perhaps brain waves are important in communicating across large distances in the brain, helping to coordinate various functions and mental experiences. Perhaps EEG will ultimately prove to be useful, even necessary, in pinpointing the neural basis of consciousness.

2. Magnetoencephalography (MEG) or Magnetic Source Imaging (MSI)

This device measures the magnetic fields that emanate from brains. Since brain cells create electrical energy, they also create an electromagnetic field. In this technique, a person's head is surrounded by especially sensitive magnetic field detectors called superconducting quantum interference devices (**SQUID**). These instruments are able to detect minute magnetic fields that are produced by the active neurons in the brain. An advantage of this technique is that MEG captures brain changes faster than other brain imaging devices; that is, it has very fast **time resolution**. Therefore, MEG is useful in capturing rapid changes that occur as a brain processes information. A drawback of this technique is its poor **spatial resolution**; MEG's ability to pinpoint the exact locations of neural activity is much worse than with other imaging tools.

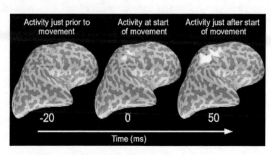

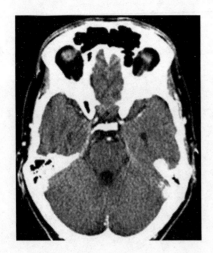

3. Computerized Axial Tomography (CAT scan or CT)

In this technique, X-rays are taken of a series of parallel planes of the brain and the results are sent to a computer that then assembles a picture of the brain based on the X-ray data. The computed image is called a **tomogram**. Unfortunately, the X-ray image is not very clear, nor does it differentiate organs and bone very well. The modern solution is to take X-rays from multiple angles and have a computer calculate the tomogram from the more dense data. This was first done in 1971 in England by Allan Cormack and Godfrey Hounsfield, who subsequently were awarded the Nobel Prize in 1979 for their accomplishment. A CAT scan can detect tumors, strokes, or other structural abnormalities because it gives a picture of brain anatomy. It does not show brain *functioning*, however, so is not as useful for localizing brain functions.

4. Positron Emission Tomography (PET scan)

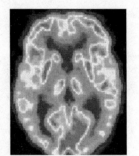

Researchers have long been using radioactive substances in animals to stain cells for X-ray examination or for later autopsy examination. These chemicals are called **radioactive tracers**. After CAT scan was developed, scientists realized that they could construct an image of the distribution of tracers in the brain. It was soon determined that blood flow was the best indicator of neuronal activity since cells use glucose for fuel, and blood will therefore automatically move to areas of rapid cell firing. The first PET scanner was developed in 1973 by Michael Ter-Pogossian at Washington University Medical School in St. Louis. Also, Michael Phelps of UCLA was awarded the U.S. government's Enrico Fermi Award for his pioneering work on PET.

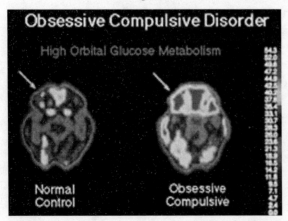

PET scan can be used to show brain activity associated with psychological disorders.

In this procedure, a subject is injected with a small dose of a radioactive isotope that has a very short half-life, meaning that it will decay rapidly into a non-radioactive substance. The isotope is absorbed into brain cells, more so in those that are most active because of the increased flow of blood to those areas. As the isotope decays, it releases positrons, positively charged electrons. These particles immediately bombard surrounding electrons, a process that annihilates them both and creates gamma rays. The gamma rays travel in opposite directions from each other and can be detected by a screen surrounding the subject's head. A computer calculates where the rays came from, and their intensity (the more gamma rays, the greater the cell activity). An image is created that can be printed or displayed on a screen.

This procedure is called a PET scan because it is based on the emission of positrons, and again the computer-produced picture is called a tomogram. The PET scan shows brain functioning, not brain structure, or anatomy; that is, we get an image of where something is happening in the brain, not a picture of brain structures. The typical procedure is to have the subject engage in some mental activity then compare that brain image to one obtained when the person was not engaging in the activity. The average of a number of subjects or a number of trials is taken in order to reduce error.

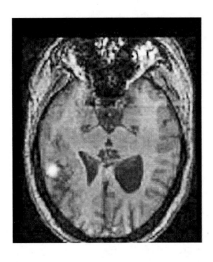

A variation of the PET scan that is less expensive is single-photon emission computed tomography (**SPECT**). While the resolution of SPECT is not as good as that of PET, the process is adequate for most distinctions in the brain. Sometimes, however, it gives an inaccurate location or too general a picture of brain activity, particularly in surgical patients where specificity is necessary. The Mayo Clinic in Rochester, Minnesota has refined a technique called **SISCOM** that uses computer software to create images that narrow the target area. SISCOM is used to help guide surgeons in removing brain tissue associated with seizures or other abnormalities.

5. Magnetic Resonance Imaging (MRI)

With the MRI technique, a person's head is surrounded by electromagnets that are used to align the magnetic fields of atoms in the brain. Radiowave pulses are then used to disturb the aligned atoms, causing them to emit radio signals in proportion to the number and state of the atoms. These emissions are known as radio frequency (RF) excitation pulses. These signals can be detected and then used by a computer to create an image of the brain.

Early machines took perhaps 20 minutes to create an image, but modern machines use "single shot" imaging in which all data is collected from a single RF excitation pulse. Today an ultrafast scan takes only a fraction of a second. MRI shows anatomical features with great clarity, providing much better resolution than does CAT scan.

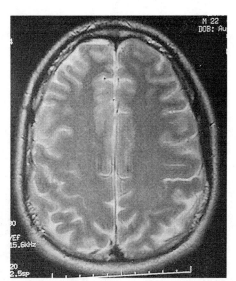

There are several variations of MRI used today to make images of a brain. One of the most common is **Diffusion Tensor Imaging** (DTI) which measures the diffusion of water in tissue. This is particularly valuable in detecting connections between brain areas, for example when damaged by stroke.

6. Functional Magnetic Resonance Imaging (fMRI)

In 1990, scientists discovered that MRI could be used to detect magnetic fluctuations that occur in the blood. By 1991, researchers showed that this procedure would work in the cells of the human brain, which receive oxygen via the blood vessels. Thus, a new use of MRI was born that was called functional MRI and commonly abbreviated fMRI. It is based on the idea of detecting the amount of oxygen in regions of the brain, indicating where brain cell firing is most active (high levels of oxygen become concentrated in areas of the brain that have high rates of neuronal firing).

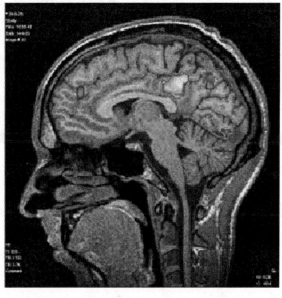

While MRI shows only brain anatomy (structure), fMRI shows brain functioning. This means that MRI can

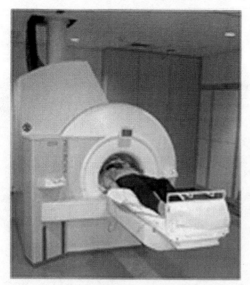

create an image of brain anatomy, but fMRI can show areas of the brain that are most active at a given moment. A subject can be asked to engage in some activity and fMRI will show which parts of the brain are involved in that activity. This technique even allows for the creation of high resolution 3D maps of the brain.

There are potential hazards of fMRI, however, including the effect of the radio pulses on brain tissue, a hazard that is regulated by the FDA. Although it is a very expensive technique, fMRI is today the best single technique of detecting where cellular activity is occurring within the living human brain, since it gives better resolution than PET.

Previously it has been difficult to use fMRI with monkeys, because they will not sit still long enough, mainly because the magnet makes loud banging noises. However, some success has recently been reported by training

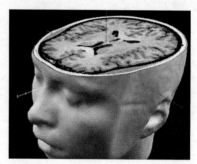

monkeys to sit patiently, by using a special seat that holds the monkey still, and by working with manufacturers to develop MRI machines with vertical magnets so that monkeys can sit upright instead of lying down. It is important to do fMRI research on monkeys because it will advance understanding in comparative biology and will help cognitive scientists make more accurate human measurements by providing clues regarding where to look for certain functions in humans.

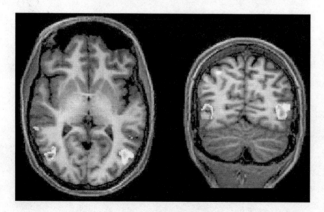

The strength of the magnetic field used by MRI is measured in teslas (T). A typical MRI is 1.5T. New machines, which give much better resolution, are 4T, which is equal to 80,000 times the Earth's magnetic field. Ohio State University has an 8T MRI capable of taking an image in 45 minutes that would normally require four hours. The University of Minnesota has a Magnetic Resonance Research Center that uses a 7T machine. Already this advanced technology is providing amazingly detailed pictures of brain activity, including images of columns of cells in the visual cortex that respond to signals from one eye or the other, which had never been imaged before. Minnesota scientists are so enthusiastic that they are predicting these new machines will take us into the most ineffable qualities of brain activity. The MRI Center director at Minnesota, Kamil Ugurbil, said, "Consciousness and identity are not so mysterious. The sum of the parts is capable of defining the whole. But will this technology have an impact on consciousness? At some point it will." But lofty aspirations and predictions only rarely culminate in success. It is easy to be optimistic when diving in to such revolutionary waters, particularly with such high powered equipment. But will it succeed? We shall see.

Latency of EROS activity: 76 ms

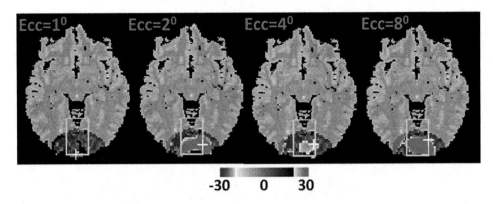

7. Event-Related Optical Signals (EROS)

Since fMRI is so expensive, some researchers are seeking a budget-conscious alternative. They have turned to light. In this new experimental procedure, a fiber optic source shines infrared light into a person's head through the scalp. The light is scattered by brain tissue, but – here's the key – it is scattered differently by neurons that are active than by those that are at rest. Therefore, a surrounding detector can determine the source, that is, the location in the brain, of cellular activity by picking up the scattered light reflections.

The resolution of EROS is about as good as EEG, and because of the low cost, this may turn out to be an important alternative to PET and fMRI. The drawback is that the light can only detect cell activity that is near the skull; EROS cannot detect activity deeper in the brain.

8. Transcranial Magnetic Stimulation (TMS)

TMS is not really an imaging technique, but is a mostly safe, non-invasive procedure that uses powerful pulsing magnetic fields to stimulate brain cells and help scientists determine the functions of brain areas. A variation known as **repetitive transcranial magnetic stimulation (rTMS)** can measure and modify the activity of brain cells, and therefore is used for various therapies.

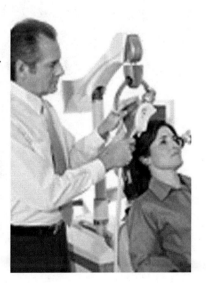

In this procedure, a powerful magnet is placed near the head, which stimulates brain cells in that region. The magnetic energy pulsates through a figure-8 shaped coil which is held near a targeted region of the patient's head. This therapy is being used to treat migraine headaches, strokes, hallucinations, and depression. Some patients with mood disorders are able to avoid **electroconvulsive therapy (ECT or shock treatment)** by using rTMS. Some comparison studies have found rTMS to be nearly equal in reducing depression as is ECT (Pridmore, 2000).

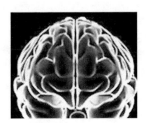

Chapter 4

HEREDITY AND GENETICS
Recipes for brains and more!

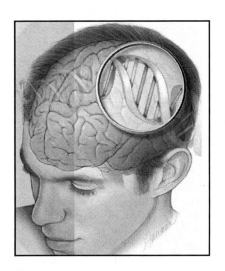

$\mathcal{S}urely\ you've\ heard$ of the **Human Genome Project**. The goal of this project was to map the complete genetic recipe of human beings. In February 2001, the two groups of scientists working on this project presented the complete findings. Surprisingly, while experts had predicted that about 100,000 genes make up the human genome, closer to 30,000 seems to be the correct number. Now, the next step is to determine what all these genes do, and then devise ways either to trigger genes to express their recipes, or to stop genes from doing what they are programmed to do. Gene therapy has already been performed on humans on a very limited scale, and in the future there undoubtedly will be significant and astounding progress in this important and amazing endeavor.

Chromosomes

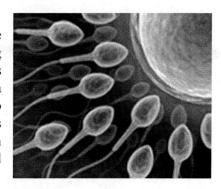

Heredity begins with a sperm and an egg. You were created by the union of a sperm cell from your father and an egg from your mother. The egg is called an **ovum** (plural = ova), and normally contains 23 chemical strands called **chromosomes**. These chromosomes were selected into the egg by a biological process (**meiosis**) that sorted a woman's 46 chromosomes into two ova with 23 in each. Likewise, in the **sperm cell** there are 23 chromosomes that were selected by meiosis from the father's 46. Chromosomes come in pairs, and one from each pair of a woman's is selected into an ovum, and one from each pair of a man's is selected into a sperm cell.

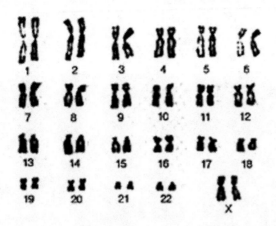

If we take any cell from your body (other than sperm or ovum), we can look at it under a powerful microscope and see your 46 chromosomes. Chromosomes come in pairs: One of each pair came from Mom, and one from Dad. So, we each have 23 pairs of chromosomes. The total set of a person's chromosomes is called a **karyotype**. A normal human karyotype has 46 chromosomes consisting of 23 from each parent. The chromosomes are different in size, and scientists use this fact to number them. The two largest chromosomes, one from dad and one from mom, are labeled #1. The next largest pair is #2. This continues for 22 pairs of chromosomes, the smallest pair termed #22. These 22 pairs of chromosomes are referred to as **autosomes**. Autosomes are the same types in men and in women. However, the two chromosomes that are not numbered are the chromosomes that determine sexual characteristics. They are different in men and women. Women have two similar **sex chromosomes**, labeled X, while men have one X and a very small chromosome labeled Y.

The recipe for genetic sex is carried by the two sex chromosomes. As mentioned, women have two sex chromosomes of the same type, called **X chromosomes**, while men have one X chromosome and a smaller **Y chromosome**; women are XX and men are XY. This is always the case in mammals – the female has two of the same type of sex chromosome while the male has two different sex chromosomes. Interestingly, in birds it is the other way around – the male bird is ZZ, while the female is ZW.

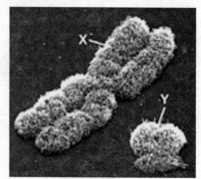

Women get one X chromosome each from mother and father. Women get 23 chromosomes from their mother, one of which is an X chromosome. Women also get 23 chromosomes from their father, and one of them is an X chromosome. So, a woman is known as XX. Men also get 23 chromosomes from their mother, including one X chromosome. But from their father, men get 23 chromosomes one of which is the smaller Y chromosome. Men are called XY. That is the typical situation.

However, it is not the chromosomes that determine sexual characteristics; rather, it is genes carried on chromosomes that program proteins to carry out various functions in the body. A gene can sometimes be located on other than its normal chromosome, and genes can be turned off or turned on. For example, about 1 in 20,000 men have no Y chromosome. Similarly, a woman could carry a Y chromosome. There are many definitions of sex, of which the genetic or chromosomal is only one. It's definitely rare, but occasionally a person is defined as male or female who does not have the corresponding typical pattern of sex chromosomes. The recipes for sexual characteristics are carried by genes, not chromosomes. However, almost always the primary sex determination genes are carried in certain addresses on the X and Y chromosomes.

Many more males are conceived than females because the sperm cells that carry a Y chromosome (androsperm) swim faster and have more pointy heads than the sperm cells that carry an X chromosome (gynosperm). However, males die more often than females at every stage of development, including prenatally. By birth, there are about 105 boys for every 100 girls, by young adulthood there are about equal numbers, and by old age there are many more women than men, which creates a social problem in old age.

Each ovum or each sperm cell that we create will contain one chromosome from each pair that we have. This process is called meiosis. So, the result is that normal germ cells (the ova and sperm) contain 23 chromosomes each. When sperm and egg unite, the fertilized egg is called a **zygote**, and contains 23 pairs, or 46 chromosomes. We refer to them as pairs because there are two of each type – one from mom and one from dad in the zygote. You were once a zygote, a long time ago. Do you remember your journey down your mother's **fallopian tube**? Remember how dark it was?

Some people did not make the journey down the fallopian tube because conception took place in a laboratory petri dish. These are popularly called test-tube babies, but scientifically the process is called in vitro ("in glass") fertilization. In these cases, mature eggs from the mother are mixed with sperm from the father in a laboratory preparation. The zygote is then implanted into the mother's womb, where it might begin to divide and grow (nearly 50% of zygotes do not make it to birth).

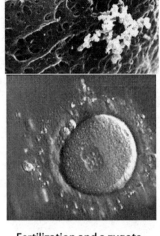

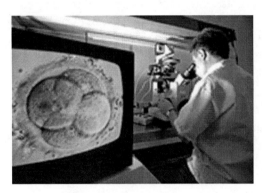

The first test-tube baby was Louise Brown, born on July 25, 1978. Today this is a common procedure at fertility clinics around the world. It is estimated that more than four million babies have been conceived this way. Robert Edwards, the British scientist whose research led to in vitro fertilization won the Nobel Prize in Medicine in 2010.

Fertilization and a zygote.

A more controversial procedure is **cytoplasmic transfer**, in which the cytoplasm that surrounds the nucleus of an egg is taken from a healthy donor and injected into the egg of an infertile woman before the egg is fertilized. Since cytoplasm has genetic material called mitochondria DNA, the resulting baby technically has three parents! However, it is controversial because a number of problems have been reported using this procedure.

Zygotes develop by copying and dividing, a process called **mitosis**. One cell becomes two, two cells become four, four become eight, and so on. Therefore, each cell in the body has a copy of the original 46 chromosomes. And eventually (after a few days) a zygote implants in the mother's uterus where further development occurs and the basic stem cells begin to differentiate into particular kinds of cells. In the first eight weeks the organism is known as an **embryo**, and from then to birth it is called a **fetus**.

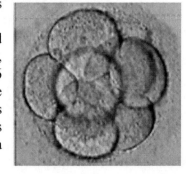

Twins

Sometimes two zygotes develop in a uterus at the same time; these are twins. Twins are divided into two types. If a woman produces two different ova at around the same time, and if two different sperm cells then fertilize those two eggs (resulting in two zygotes), the zygotes will develop into **fraternal twins**, which scientifically are called **dizygotic twins** ("two-egg" twins).

MZ twins (top) often look very similar, but can have differences because their environments are not the same, and even their genes are not exactly the same due to tiny errors that occur during mitosis. DZ twins (bottom) can be very much unlike one another!

On the other hand, if a single zygote should separate into two, then **identical twins** will result. They are called **monozygotic twins** ("one-egg" twins). **MZ** twins are virtually identical in their genetic recipes, since they came from one egg and one sperm cell, while **DZ** twins have somewhat different genes similar to siblings.

DZ twins result when two different eggs are fertilized by two different sperm cells. The sperm cells don't even need to come from the same man (although of course they nearly always do). Also, the fertilization could take place in a laboratory, and the fertilized eggs (the zygotes) could then be implanted into a carrier woman. DZ twins need not be very much alike in genetic inheritance! Of course, DZ twins normally have the same parents, so share 25% of their chromosomes on the average.

MZ twins result from one fertilized egg – one ovum is fertilized by one sperm cell, but then, after copying the 46 chromosomes, the single fertilized cell splits into two zygotes that have the same chromosomes (or, nearly the same, since some small errors occur in copying). Notice that MZ twins, therefore, have the exact same chromosomes as each other (except for biological variations and errors that occur). DZ twins can be of different genders, but MZ twins must be the same gender since they have the same chromosomes.

Psychologists study MZ twins raised together compared to MZ twins raised apart in an attempt to find degrees of heritability of various traits. They are also compared to DZ twins. The degree to which twins are alike in a certain trait is called the **concordance rate**. For instance, the concordance rate for schizophrenia in MZ twins is about 50%. This means that when one twin has schizophrenia, about half the time the other twin also has schizophrenia.

Sometimes a rare event happens with MZ twins. A zygote is formed by fertilization of egg and sperm, it then undergoes mitosis and a copy is made, the two cells pull away from each other forming MZ twins, and then the two cells are pulled back together only in one part of their membrane. There is a kind of biological glue that holds cells together, but sometimes the glue fails and we get MZ twins. However, in rare cases the glue pulls the two cells back together in one mirror-image part of the cell. The result is **conjoined twins**; MZ twins who are joined at one part of the body. A famous pair of conjoined twins from Siam (the former name for the country of Thailand) was Chang and Eng; hence, we got the erroneous term Siamese twins.

These conjoined twins share a body with each controlling one side, and yet they are able to attend college, play sports, and even drive a car.

It's amazing, but apparently twins can be formed in some unusual, very rare, conditions other than by DZ or MZ. It was found, for example, that twins can be created by two sperm cells fusing with one ovum. The result is known as **semi-identical twins**. This type of twin is halfway between DZ and MZ in genetic similarity. Even more rare are human chimeras. The term "chimera" comes from Greek mythology and refers to an animal that has a mix of parts of different animals. A **human chimera** is formed when two zygotes fuse together; that is, two DZ twins merge into one zygote. The cells of this person's body will show different genes. This is very rare; there are only about 40 known reported cases. On the other hand, as many as 8% of DZ twins are **blood chimeras** because they got some genetic material in their blood from their twin when developing in the womb since they shared some of the same placenta.

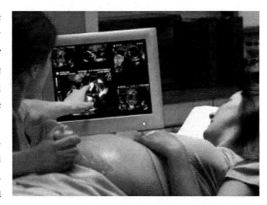

An interesting oddity is **vanishing twin syndrome**. When twins are formed in the early prenatal period, one of them may receive the bulk of nutrients while the other shrinks and dies. At birth, it may easily go undetected that there originally was a twin. If this happens early in the pregnancy, the vanishing twin is absorbed or miscarried, but in the second or third trimester, serious problems could result. Some estimates have suggested that as many as six percent of single births originated as twins or multiple embryos. In fact, maybe you had a twin who vanished!

Because many more women are now having ultrasounds during pregnancy, there is more identification of vanishing twin syndrome, which was not noticed in most cases in the past. This can lead to a feeling of loss if a couple was expecting twins.

Genes

If we look at chromosomes up close, we see that they are long strands of a chemical called deoxyribonucleic acid, or **DNA**. This chemical is often called the molecule of life. It is shaped like a **double helix**, two spirals wound around each other, like a twisted ladder (or two intertwined slinkys). Connecting the two spirals (like the rungs of a ladder) are pairs of chemicals hooked together called **base pairs**. There are only four chemical bases in the DNA molecule: Adenine (**A**), Thymine (**T**), Cytosine (**C**), and Guanine (**G**). These base chemicals always pair up a certain way: A always goes with T, and C always goes with G. (Remember: <u>A</u>lways <u>T</u>ogether, and <u>C</u>losely <u>G</u>lued). This arrangement allows for easy reproduction.

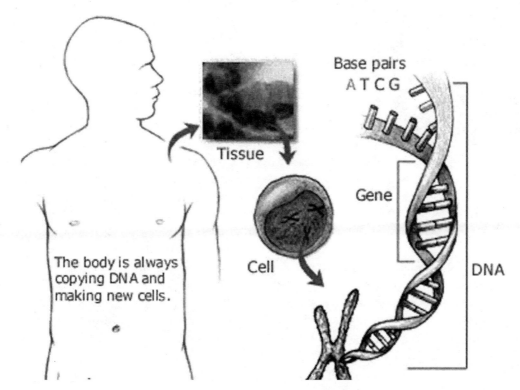

The body is always copying DNA and making new cells.

Tissue

Cell

Base pairs
A T C G

Gene

DNA

When the long chromosome divides (unzips down its middle), the DNA sequence can easily be replicated by replacing the appropriate chemicals in each case. Where there is an A, put a T. Where there is a T, put an A. Where there is a C, put a G. Where there is a G, put a C. Because of this copying process, all the cells in your body contain chromosomes that have the same sequence of base pairs as in the original chromosomes you received from your parents. The sequence of bases (A, T, C, and G) that is in your chromosomes is the genetic recipe for you – your genome.

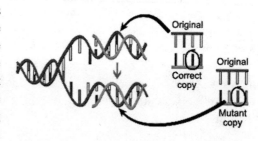

A particular sequence of base pairs on a chromosome might have a biological job to do. That sequence is then called a **gene**. Genes, then, are segments of chromosomes that consist of a particular sequence of bases that represents a recipe for the body. A gene sequence will be something like: ACGGGTCAATTCAGCAGCAGC… but very, very long. Combinations of three base pairs (for example, CAG) are recipes for certain body proteins and often come in long repeating chains. When chromosomes are passed from generation to generation and are replicated, mistakes often happen. These mistakes are called **mutations**. There are many types of mutations; for example, a T could be replaced by a C, but in each case they result in changes in the gene's normal, stable sequence.

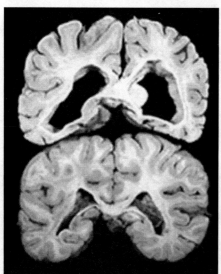

A Huntington's brain at top compared to a normal brain at bottom.

Certain neurological problems are produced when a series of three base pairs on the gene repeats itself too much. These genetic errors are known as **triplet** (or **trinucleotide**) **repeat** mutations (or expansions). Three base pairs in a row is a recipe for a certain protein, for example, CTG. But three in a row can repeat itself over and over many times in mutations. For example, abnormally long CAG repeats have been found to be associated with a number of neurodegenerative disorders, including **Huntington's disease**, which occurs when there are about 40 or more CAG repeats on a section of chromosome #4. The number of trinucleotide repeats can increase when passed from one generation to the next, resulting in each generation suffering the corresponding medical condition earlier and more severely than the previous generation. Other examples of conditions influenced by the triplet repeats are abnormal finger and toe development and several spinal cerebellar ataxias.

In Huntington's disease, if CAG appears a small number of times, a person is normal, while if CAG repeats a large number of times, then the person has a mutation that produces a disease. As men age, their sperm cells divide many times, increasing the risk of mutations. For example, men over 50 have three times the chance of having a baby with schizophrenia compared to younger men (Malaspina, 2001).

Another interesting example is **Williams syndrome**, a rare genetic disorder that causes a number of problems including cognitive difficulties (Bellugi, 2007). In this condition, people resemble one another in an elfin-like manner, love music and have a talent for it, have heart problems, age prematurely, have severe difficulty with spatial perception, and are intellectually delayed. Despite their problems, children with Williams syndrome excel at language and social skills. Their language ability is extraordinarily good – precisely the opposite of autistic children. This finding indicates that language and cognitive skills are at least somewhat separate in the brain.

Williams syndrome is caused by a **deletion** that occurs when a group of genes on chromosome #7 is deleted during embryonic development. Interestingly, a gene on chromosome #7 has recently been discovered that apparently influences language ability (Monaco, 2001). A mutation in this gene causes problems in grammar and pronunciation.

The most common form of inherited intellectual disability is **fragile X syndrome**. Affecting boys twice as often as girls, it is the result of a mutated gene on the X chromosome in which the trinucleotide CGG repeats more than 200 times causing loss of a protein that is

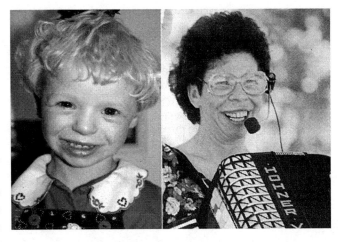

abundant in the brain. A gene with between 50 and 200 CGG repeats is called a **permutation**, and carriers will not have the full range of symptoms, though symptoms such as tremors, loss of balance, and diminished IQ scores may develop in old age (Hagerman, 2002). Similar mutations involving repeats or deletions of DNA segments have been found in disorders such as schizophrenia, autism, and attention deficit/hyperactivity disorder (ADHD).

If a person inherits the same gene from mother and father, then the term **homozygous** is used with regard to that gene or trait. If the genes are different, then it is called **heterozygous**. Since we receive genes from both parents, sometimes there is a conflict in the recipes and we are heterozygous for a particular gene. One gene codes for brown eyes and the other for blue eyes, for instance. Or, one gene codes for cystic fibrosis and the other gene is normal. When this happens, sometimes our bodies combine the two recipes, for example in determining blood types. But it is more common when genes are heterozygous for our bodies to follow one genetic recipe and ignore the other. The gene that is followed is called **dominant** and the gene that is ignored is called **recessive**.

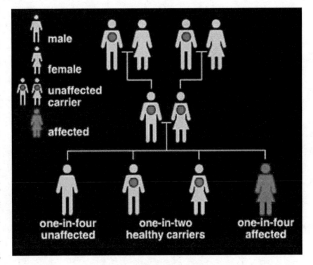

Therefore, in order to have a recessive trait, you would need to inherit a recessive gene from each parent, since if you got a dominant gene from either parent, you would have the dominant trait. Huntington's disease, the fatal brain disease that shows up late in life, is caused by a dominant gene on chromosome #4. On the other hand, albinism, cystic fibrosis, and blue eyes are recessive traits. Therefore, we need only inherit the gene for Huntington's from one parent to express this disease. But to have albinism, cystic fibrosis, or blue eyes we must inherit the respective recessive genes from both parents in order to show any of these traits.

An exception involves genes on the X chromosome, since men get only one. A recessive gene on the X chromosome will not be expressed in women who have a dominant gene on their other X chromosome. However, a recessive gene on the X chromosome in a man will always be expressed because he does not have another X chromosome with the possibility of a dominant gene. Such traits are more common in men; they inherit the gene from their mothers, who usually do not have the trait. For a woman to have such a recessive trait, she would need to inherit the recessive gene from both her parents (meaning her father has the trait). Such traits are called **sex-linked** or **X-linked**, and include red-green color blindness, hemophilia, and baldness.

It is important to recognize that what is inherited are chemical recipes called genes. These genes act like blueprints for the body to develop proteins, the building blocks for anatomy and physiology. We do not directly inherit our characteristics; rather, we inherit the recipes for our characteristics.

The recipe that we inherit is known as our **genotype**, while the totality of actual physical characteristics, qualities, and traits that we show is called our **phenotype**. You don't get every recipe that you inherit. Some genes are

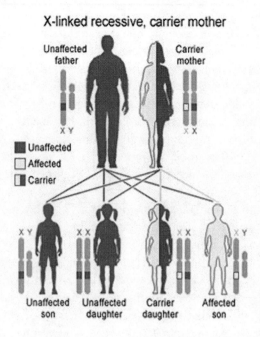

recessive, and some genes aren't expressed. Two people with the same phenotype, say, brown eyes, might have different genotypes. That is, the recipes might be different but they result in the same trait that is exhibited.

Chromosome Abnormalities

Sometimes errors occur in the number of chromosomes that are selected into the **germ cells**, the ovum or the sperm. Typically when an ovum or a sperm cell has the wrong number of chromosomes (should be 23), the cell will not develop to maturity. However, some of these cells do mature, and the result is a person with a different number of chromosomes than the typical 46. These cases are known as **chromosome abnormalities**.

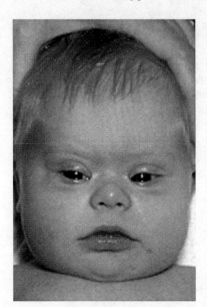

Down syndrome.

The most common error is when an extra chromosome #21 gets into the sperm or egg via an error in the process of meiosis. The embryo then has three chromosomes #21, for a total of 47 chromosomes. This condition is called **Down syndrome**. The result is intellectual disability and a number of other physical problems. This mistake in chromosome selection becomes more likely as people age, so older men and women have a higher risk that their newborns will have Down syndrome. There are tests that can be done during pregnancy, such as removing cells from the fetus and looking at them under a microscope that can detect Down syndrome far in advance of birth.

Another chromosome error involves the sex chromosomes. A woman may receive more than two X chromosomes, for example. When a woman has too many sex chromosomes, the condition is called **superfemale**. A man might receive more than one Y chromosome, also. When a man has too many Y chromosomes the condition is called **supermale**. Another error occurs when a woman has only has one X chromosome; that condition is called **Turner's**

syndrome. Finally, if a person has two X chromosomes and a Y chromosome the condition is called **Klinefelter's syndrome**.

A person with Klinefelter's syndrome (XXY) will develop some female characteristics, such as enlarged breasts, but some male characteristics because of the Y chromosome. In fact, all of the chromosome abnormalities that involve the sex chromosomes involve physical conditions, including problems in sexual maturation, such as infertility. As noted, in Klinefelter's syndrome a person has a mix of male and female characteristics. Women with Turner's syndrome are short, do not develop sexually, and have heart and kidney problems. In chromosome-land, more is not better; 46 is the right number. Any other number can be a problem.

Turner's syndrome (X0).

The On-Off Switch

A different situation sometimes arises when the Y chromosome does not turn on – does not express its genes. A person can inherit the recipe for being male – an XY pattern – but because of an error in expression of the Y chromosome, the person ends up with female characteristics. This is not a chromosome abnormality. For example, in a condition called **androgen insensitivity**, a person has the XY genotype, but the cells of the person's body do not react to the male hormones triggered by the Y chromosome. Hence, the person ends up with a female phenotype. This woman has the chromosomal recipe for being male, but the recipe was not carried out, so she is female.

A converse situation occurs in **congenital adrenal hyperplasia** (CAH). This person has the XX chromosome pattern of a female, but because the adrenal glands are not working properly the person is exposed to high levels of male hormones and a penis develops. This condition can be corrected with prenatal medications if detected early. These cases show that genes do not necessarily determine cellular outcomes. Genes act like recipes that can be turned on or turned off, and can be affected by other factors.

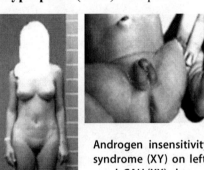

Androgen insensitivity syndrome (XY) on left, and CAH (XX) above.

The various factors that influence the expression of a gene are called **transcription factors**. These include other genes, hormones, and experiences. The study of **epigenetics** attempts to discover the role of transcription factors. Epigenetic research has shown, for example, that the heritability of eating disorders does not become significant until after puberty (Culbert, 2009). In younger girls, heredity is not a strong factor in disordered eating. However, after puberty, disordered eating has a high heritability. Something about puberty (likely the hormone levels) influences the expression of genes that then influence eating disorders.

Genes can be turned on and turned off. Some genes play this role; their job is to moderate other genes. Experience in the world, such as trauma, can cause the body to release hormones that, too, can be influential in gene expression. This concept explains why MZ twins can be different in phenotype, though they have the same genotype. The same genes do not necessarily result in the same physical conditions because genes can be turned on or turned off by experiences.

Nature vs. Nurture

One of the common questions in psychology is to what extent we are shaped by our heredity and to what extent we are shaped by experience. This is the **nature-nurture** issue that was a major question in the early days of psychology, and continues even today. This is something of a false, or at least, a misleading, question. It is silly to deny that either nature or nurture is a significant contributor to our psychological lives. It is equally silly to try to divide them. Should we ask to what extent the images on our computer screen are due to hardware and what extent to software? Should we ask if the taste of our food is due to the recipe or the ingredients? When reading the words in this sentence, would it be helpful to know how much is contributed by ink and how much by paper? Of course, the words you are reading here right now are produced by ink absorbed into paper – ink and paper working together. In a similar fashion, our physical and psychological characteristics are formed by our genes being absorbed into our experiences. It is the *interaction* between genes and environment that is important. Genes are expressed in certain ways depending on certain conditions. Genes and environment interact.

These two things – heredity and experience – both affect us, and they are intertwined together. For example, in their analysis of language acquisition, Karmiloff and Karmiloff-Smith (2001) argue that nature and nurture are so intertwined and dependent on each other that debate about their relative influences is not worthwhile. We are not born with everything we will have; we develop. Yes, at conception we receive a recipe, a potential. But, that recipe is malleable and flexible. It also comes with a clock. The genes we inherit will express themselves at different times and to different degrees. Often we carry genes for traits that will never be expressed (for example, recessive genes). Also, experiences might provide for genetic expression, or they might not. A genetic predisposition might not be fulfilled because of the lack of environmental stimuli to bring it out.

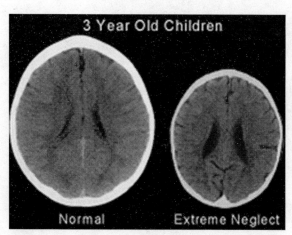

3 Year Old Children

Normal   Extreme Neglect

Neglect and abuse in childhood are environmental factors that can adversely affect brain development.

For instance, children who were abused in childhood will often later develop psychological disorders, but not always. A gene on the X chromosome was discovered that helps explain this difference (Caspi, 2002). Having a certain gene and experiencing abuse will lead to development of a disorder, but having a different gene together with abuse does not lead to disorder. Maltreatment early in life can cause relatively permanent changes in brain chemistry. A child's brain becomes hypersensitive to danger and threats because of early abuse. Such a child later in life might respond to a stressful situation with anxiety, escape, or depression because his or her brain has become overly sensitized (Caspi, 2010).

A similar pattern can occur with the development of severe depression or alcoholism. A person might have the genetic potential to develop these disorders, but never have an experience that turns on the genes. For instance, researchers have identified a gene that together with a traumatic experience will result in depression or alcoholism (Philibert, 2008). The study's lead author, Robert Philibert, said, "Genes, in conjunction with a person's exposure to different life experiences and environments, play a role in depression, even though all the specific mechanisms by which this happens are not well understood. This study gave us some interesting information about one specific mechanism."

The same research lab also identified a gene that appears to make people more likely to develop an addiction to cigarette smoking (Philibert, 2009).

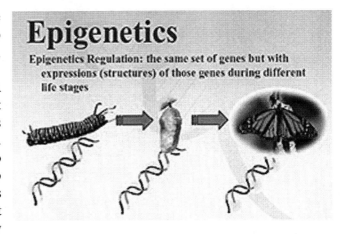

In another case, Frank Gilliland at UCLA found a gene that explains why when a pregnant mother smokes sometimes her child later develops asthma, and sometimes does not (Wang, 2008). Also, researchers have noticed that people tend to drink more alcohol when they are with others who are drinking a lot; but, they found that this effect is modulated by a certain gene (Larsen, 2010). That is, if you have a certain gene you will be less likely influenced by excessive drinking going on around you. Researchers who study schizophrenia have speculated that schizophrenia may be the result of genes interacting with a virus (Moises, 2002). There are many such examples of how heredity and experience interact and complement each other. The nature-nurture issue is based on a false assumption that these are two separate categories. Nature and nurture interact.

Gimme a "G", Gimme an "E"

Researchers studying **gene-environment interaction** (G x E) are uncovering some specifics about the process. For example, it was discovered that boys with a specific gene that affects the dopamine process in the brain were less likely to develop depression when rejected by their mothers than were boys who did not have the gene (Haeffel, 2008). Previous research has shown that genes can influence depression, and that aversive parenting can influence depression, but here is a good example of G x E. Psychological characteristics are produced by brain functioning involving numerous chemicals and neural pathways. These brain states can be moderated or influenced by both genetic factors and environmental factors. The future trend in psychology will be to find ways in which specific genes interact with specific experiences to produce psychological conditions.

Nature and nurture are interdependent. Normal development depends on certain experiences in the world. For example, babies are genetically programmed to see a certain way – to see colors, shapes, forms, movement, and so on; but, this genetic programming requires experience to be realized. If deprived of light and visual experiences, the cells of the eye and brain will not develop normally, and vision will not manifest its genetic destiny. LeGrand (2004) found that people who were visually deprived early in life later did not process faces in a holistic manner, which brains normally do.

There are tons of other examples of how deprivation can interfere with genetic potential. For instance, experiences in the world influence learning. Brains are genetically designed to learn – to change with experience – that is the result of millions of years of evolution of the brain; brains can learn, can change with experience, can be programmed. But the genes that influence brain development, architecture, and physiology, are also intertwined with environmental experience. Alcohol consumption during pregnancy, for example, interferes with the genetic formula for brain development. Also, certain experiences later in life will have greater or lesser effects on different people because of their genetic endowment. One person will be sensitive, another resilient. It is futile to try to separate these two influences, genetics and learning, since they are intricately interwoven and dependent on each other.

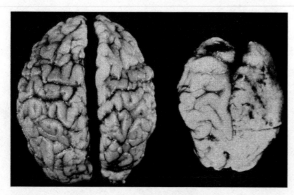

The brains of 6 week old babies: normal (left) and fetal alcohol syndrome (right).

Heredity gives us a blueprint for development. But experience influences how we develop. This interaction is often easiest to describe with examples of how experiences interfere with heredity's recipe. For instance, **teratogens** (Greek for "causes monsters") are substances that disturb normal prenatal development. Alcohol is one; it can cross the placental barrier and damage fetal development, causing **fetal alcohol syndrome**.

PKU (phenylketonuria) is a condition in which a person cannot metabolize an ingredient in food called phenylalanine. This inability is determined by a recessive gene. You might be a carrier of PKU but not have the disorder; that would require getting the PKU gene from both parents, which is somewhat rare. Children with PKU who eat normal foods, such as milk, that contain phenylalanine will have damage to the cells of their body, including brain cells, resulting in intellectual disability. Both the gene and experience contribute. A low IQ score can be prevented by either changing the gene, or changing the diet. Since we cannot yet alter this particular gene, the solution is to test babies for PKU and if they are positive, then put them on a special diet low in phenylalanine. Notice that if a child has intellectual disability from PKU, we can either blame the gene or the food – both explanations are half right; it's neither nature nor nurture, but an interaction between them.

Every bit of us, our physical and psychological beings, are the result of the dance between these two inseparable forces. We develop; we are neither born with anything, nor learn anything, entirely. It is the interaction between the two that makes us unfold the way we do. Heredity matters, but, so does experience. These two forces interact. We are the sum of our parts, and more: We are the interactions of our parts.

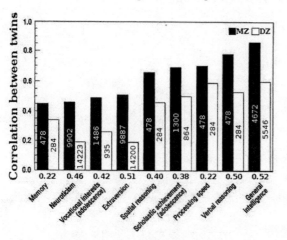

Estimated trait heritability.

Modern Gene Research

Contemporary scientists have discovered genes that influence over 100 neurological disorders and many mental disorders. Such research is known as **gene linkage analysis**. However, while occasionally a trait is influenced by only one gene, as in the case of Huntington's disease, nearly always our psychological characteristics are influenced by a large number of genes. Such traits are called **polygenic**.

For instance, several genes have been identified that make a person at risk for developing Alzheimer's disease. Schizophrenia, one of the most serious psychotic disturbances, is known to be influenced by several genes, including dysbindin, DISC-1, DAO, neuregulin 1, and neuregulin 3. The dysbindin gene was recently found to affect intelligence, and can be added to the list of many different genes that have been shown to influence learning

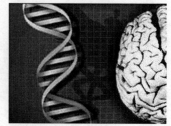

and memory (Burdick, 2006). There are so many genes now known that predispose a person to the development of various traits that it is possible today to have your genome examined in a laboratory and get a report detailing the level of risk you have for developing hundreds of diseases and conditions. Currently, this procedure is very expensive; but in a few years the cost will be low enough to entice millions of people to look at their genetic susceptibilities.

Regarding the brain, there are thousands of genes that contribute recipes for its anatomy and physiology. **Genetic engineering** is one area of research for determining the inheritance of traits. In one such procedure, a foreign gene is inserted into a mouse embryo. The gene will show up only in some of the mouse's cells. After mating cycles, the gene will enter the sperm and ova of mice. These **transgenic mice** can then be observed to see what effect the new gene has on their traits.

Another procedure is a bit of the opposite approach: In **knockout mice** a mutation is introduced to interfere with a gene's functions. By making a gene inactive, scientists can then study the mice to see which traits, behaviors, or conditions are abnormal since the gene is not functioning. It is also possible to mess with a gene's ability to construct proteins using **antisense RNA**, a drug that interferes with production of proteins by the gene.

These genetic engineering procedures are leading to many discoveries of what role genes play in brain development. Some results of this research are already transferring into treatments for human diseases. For example, antisense drugs are being developed to treat autoimmune diseases, and gene transfer therapy has been successful in treating a genetic immune disorder called SCID-X1, the condition the public knows as "bubble baby."

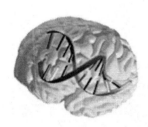

Genes, of course, are the recipes for the brain and its chemicals, therefore genes influence all of our psychological processes via the brain. In nearly every case, however, genes that have been discovered – genes for schizophrenia, Alzheimer's, learning, OCD, memory, dyslexia, personality, etc. – are only partially influential for a particular trait or condition, and are clearly working with other genes, hormones, biological events, and our experiences in the world in determining the expression of a psychological function. For example, the lead researcher of the team that discovered the dysbindin gene's influence on intelligence said, "While our data suggests the dysbindin gene influences variation in human cognitive ability and intelligence, it only explained a small proportion of it – about 3 percent. This supports a model involving multiple genetic and environmental influences on intelligence" (Burdick, 2006).

And so it is in so many cases. Genes are important contributors, but the degree to which they contribute to a psychological process can vary tremendously. It's important to acknowledge that because genes help to shape, form, and regulate our brains, they therefore are significant players in our quest to understand emotions, behaviors, and cognitive processes.

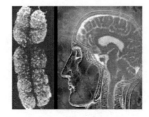

Chapter 5

BRAIN CELLS
What's with all the sparking and squirting?

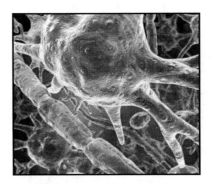

$\mathcal{A}$s with all living things, the basic unit of a brain is a cell. Blood is made of cells, livers are made of cells, bones are made of cells, skin is made of cells, and brains are made of cells. But brain cells are different from other cells because they evolved to have the ability to receive and send signals. They are like little switches that can be turned on and off. They are connected to one another in vast **neural networks** that act like a circuit board or computer software. Brain cells receive chemical signals, carry the signal a short or long distance in the brain or body by means of a change in their electric potential, and then they relay the signal to other cells using chemicals. The brain is an enormous communication system, both chemical and electrical.

There are several different kinds of cells in a brain. However, the fundamental unit of communication in the brain and in the nervous system is the **neuron**. There are billions of neurons in the human brain. They are surrounded and nourished by another type of cell called a **glial cell** (Greek for "glue" and pronounced "GLEE-ul"). To some small extent the glial cells help the neurons communicate, but mostly glial cells do the housework and clean-up necessary to keep the nervous system functioning.

The Neuron

Neurons were first described by Spanish doctor **Santiago Ramón y Cajal** (pronounced "eee-KA-YHALL") (1852-1934), who made exquisite drawings of them, and called neurons "the butterflies of the soul." Neurons come in different shapes and sizes, but they have certain similarities. The basic components of a neuron are: the cell body or **soma**, which includes the **nucleus** (Latin for "kernel") housing the **chromosomes**; and, growing out of the soma

Neurons in the back of the eye, drawn by Ramón y Cajal.

are the **dendrites**, tiny branches that extend out of the neuron in order to receive signals; and, a long branch that extends out of the soma, the **axon**, which carries a message to another location; and finally, at the end of the axon are the **terminals**, branches that send the neuron's signal to a muscle, an organ, or to another neuron by releasing chemicals. So, the dendrites receive a message, the axon carries it to another location, and then the terminals send a message to a muscle or to another neuron.

dendrites = receive   axons = carry   terminals = send

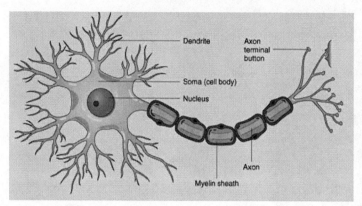

Brain cells can be damaged and die, of course. Dead neurons do not come back to life. For many years scientists believed that a brain could not create new neurons to replace those that were lost. But modern research has discovered this is not true (Gage, 1999). Even in mature adult brains, new neurons are produced in several regions such as the **hippocampus** (learning and memory center) and the **olfactory bulb** (smell area of the brain). This new growth is called **neurogenesis**. The newly created cells migrate out to other brain regions, such as the frontal lobe, where they apparently are used for learning and memory (Shors, 2001). However, some research shows that new cells can in some cases actually eliminate old memories (Feng, 2001). Also, neurogenesis apparently is related to anxiety and depression, is reduced by stress and depression, and possibly is rejuvenated by antidepressant medicines (Santarelli, 2003).

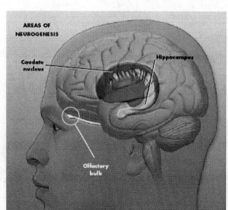

Neurogenesis has also been found in the brains of adult monkeys (Gould, 1999) and even in birds' brains (Scharff, 2000). It is estimated that you grow about 5,000 new brain cells per day; but, the majority will die unless you use them for learning (so, keep reading!). However, current research shows that only certain regions of the brain can grow new neurons, and that only one type of neuron is generated; for example, brains do not grow new sensory cells. Neurogenesis can be now be witnessed in the living brain by using a brain imaging technique that can detect chemical differences in the new cells (Swaminathan, 2007). These findings, of course, are giving some hope to researchers who are searching for treatments or cures for brain injuries and brain diseases, such as **Alzheimer's** and **Parkinson's**.

Neural Communication

A neuron has two methods of communication; one is electrical in nature. The electrical signal is created by the movement of electrically charged particles (**ions**) in and out of the neuron. This electrical process is responsible for moving a signal from one end of the neuron (the dendrites and the soma) to the other end (the terminals). That is, an electrical message is created by the movement of ions in and out of the cell, and this electrical signal travels from one end of a neuron to the other end.

The second process is chemical, which is used when a neuron sends a signal to a muscle or to another neuron, or when a neuron receives a signal from light in the eyes, or sound in the ears, or touch on the skin, or pain, or from another neuron, for example. The dendrites of a neuron have chemicals on their surface called **receptors** that are responsive to other chemicals. The dendrites receive a message via a chemical reaction when the receptors are stimulated. That chemical reaction starts the electrical process (ions moving into the cell). The electrical change in energy begins at the dendrites and moves down the axon to the terminals. When the electrical signal reaches the end of the neuron, then chemicals are squirted out. The released chemicals are called **neurotransmitters**. A chemical reaction then takes place at the receiving cell or muscle as the neurotransmitter binds with receptors on the receiving dendrites.

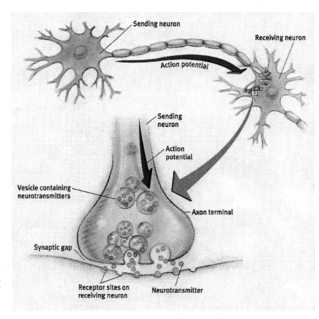

So, an electrical process is responsible for signals traveling within a neuron, while chemical reactions are responsible for signals traveling between neurons. The transmission within a neuron is called **axonal**, and is an electrical process. The transmission between neurons is called a **synapse**, and is a chemical process.

Axonal Transmission

Neurons exist in a medium of water. The water in our bodies is not tap water or Perriér. In our bodies, we have salt water – like the ocean. Suspended in the water are particles, dissolved salts, for example. Particles such as **chloride (Cl⁻)** that have more electrons than protons are said to have a **negative** charge. **Sodium (Na⁺)**, on the other hand, has a **positive** charge, because it has more protons than electrons. Both of these are greatly involved in the transmission of signals within neurons. **Potassium (K⁺)**, **calcium (Ca⁺)**, and other molecules are also involved. As mentioned above, these electrically charged particles are called **ions**.

Ions exist inside and outside a neuron. A signal travels down a neuron's axon because of a change in the electrical potential of the cell. The inside of the cell becomes more positively charged because positively charged sodium ions enter the cell. This change in electric potential starts at the cell body and continues down the axon to the terminals. The process is known as **axonal transmission**.

Open the Gates

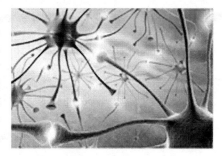

When a neuron is at rest, not being stimulated, it has a certain arrangement of ions within and around it. A neuron has a surface, a **membrane**, that can be penetrated by certain small particles, but not by large particles. There are **channels** on the surface of the neuron that ions can pass through. However, ions cannot pass through their channels at all times. The channels have **gates** on them that can open or close to allow ions to enter or leave the inside of the neuron, or to prevent them from entering or leaving. The surface membrane of a neuron is called **semipermeable** because sometimes ions can enter or leave, and sometimes they cannot.

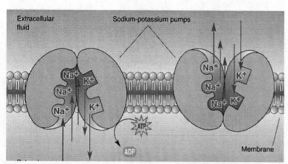

Large negative ions, called <u>anions</u>, are trapped inside the neuron. Sodium and potassium ions, on the other hand, can move through their ion channels when the gates are open. However, the neuron has a **sodium pump** that regularly moves the positively charged sodium ions out of the cell. The result is that a neuron at rest, when it is not sending a signal, has a negative charge on the inside. This is called the **resting potential** of the neuron. It measures about **−70 millivolts** (a millivolt is a thousandth of a volt; abbreviated mv). So, the inside of a neuron that is resting, that is not firing, has a tiny negative electrical charge. Because there is an electrical difference between the outside of the neuron (more positively charged) and the inside of the neuron (more negatively charged) while the cell is at rest, the neuron is called **polarized** (meaning there are two poles or extremes). Positive on the outside, negative on the inside = polarized!

The dendrites of a neuron have chemicals – receptors – on their surface that respond to other chemicals, such as those released by another neuron, or those that come from outside our body and contact the cells in our eyes, ears, nose, skin, etc. When a dendrite has a chemical reaction, it causes the gates of the neuron membrane channels to open. Since the inside of the neuron is negatively charged, sodium ions will then enter the cell. When the ion channels open up, the sodium ions want to join the party inside the cell, because of the more negative charge inside. (In electricity, this is known as opposites attracting. In humans, by the way, opposites do not normally attract. The phrase is wrong because positive and negative charges are not opposites; they complement each other. We should say, "Complements attract." That might even be true about humans!)

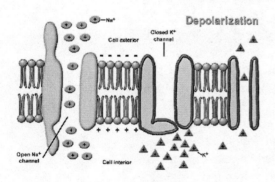

As positively charged sodium ions enter the cell, naturally, the inside of the cell gradually becomes more positively charged. We say that the cell is experiencing **depolarization**, meaning it is becoming less polarized. The electrical potential inside the neuron goes up to −69mv, then to −68mv, then −67mv, and so on. When the electric charge inside the soma reaches a certain point, called the **threshold**, then the gates controlling the channels on the axon open up.

When the gates of the channels on the axon open, sodium ions enter the axon. This causes the gates next door to open. Sodium ions enter there. Then the next gates open. Sodium enters. And so on. All the way from the soma to the terminals, the inside of the neuron is becoming more positively charged, one section at a time. The whole process takes only a split second and is known as an **action potential**. An action potential is a wave of positive electrical charge traveling from the cell body down the axon to the terminals. The cell has depolarized.

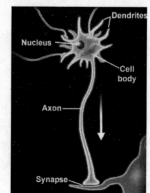

When an action potential occurs, we then say that the neuron has **fired**. The electrical charge inside the neuron goes up to about +30mv because the sodium ions are entering so furiously. Party! Party! The cell becomes completely depolarized. Then,

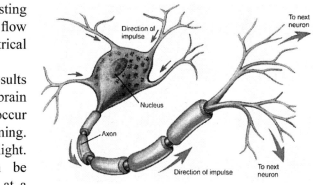

after firing, the cell returns to its negatively charged resting potential because positively charged potassium ions flow out of the channels. The cell continues to change electrical charge from negative to positive to negative, etc.

Brains are electrical machines. A **seizure** results when there is an abnormality in the electrical firing of brain cells. Many things can cause a seizure; often they occur spontaneously because of internal biological functioning. However, seizures also can be caused by a flickering light.

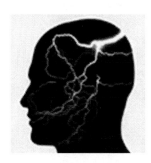

Flash-induced seizures can be produced by light flickering at a rate of 15 to 20 times per second. In 1997 hundreds of children in Japan suffered seizures while watching a Pokémon cartoon on TV. Seizures also have been caused by video games. Dramas and performances that use strobe lights often warn audience members in advance.

By the way, **novocaine** (you get it at the dentist) and similar anesthetic drugs work by blocking the sodium channels so that ions cannot enter the cell and therefore cannot send the pain signal to the brain. Thus, your mouth feels numb. Later, the novocaine wears off and the sodium channels are free to admit sodium ions into the cell. Yikes, pain! There are natural chemicals that block ion channels, too. Some sushi diners enjoy the puffer fish because it gives a tingling sensation in the mouth, the result of tetrodoxin blocking ion channels. Too much puffer fish has resulted in the deaths of daring sushi diners. Venom from snakes, cone snails, and scorpions has similar neurotoxin effects by blocking or opening ion channels.

The Going Rate

Neurons are constantly firing: Negative, positive, negative, positive, negative, positive …that is the life of a neuron. Once an action potential begins, the signal travels all the way down to the end of the axon, to the terminals. The signal cannot go part of the way, or be only partial in strength. The signal goes all the way, and at full strength. This is called the **all-or-none law**. Every action potential, every firing of a particular neuron, is the same. What differs is the *rate* of firing. The rate is different for different intensities of stimuli. Suppose a bee stings your toe. Neural signals are sent to your brain. How much pain do you feel? That depends on a number of things, but one of the most important is the rate at which those neurons from the toe are firing. A slow rate of firing means a weak stimulus, and therefore not much pain. A strong stimulus will fire the neurons at a faster rate, resulting in a more intense feeling of pain. How bright is a light? A bright light will fire the neurons in your eye at a faster rate than will a dim light. So, your brain perceives the brightness of light based on how fast the neurons are firing.

Mature neurons are covered with an insulating, fatty substance called **myelin** that is white in color. Neurons look gray. When we look at the surface of a brain we see gray matter. But the axons of those cells look white, because of the myelin. When we look at a mature spinal cord, or look at the interior of the brain, we see white matter.

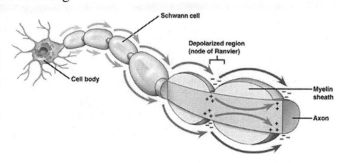

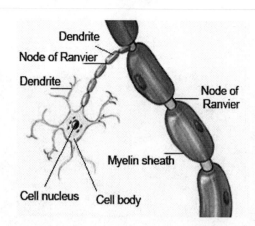

Myelin surrounds portions of the axon in clumps. At one time scientists believed that the complete axon was coated with myelin, hence the covering was called a **myelin sheath** (a sheath is a coating, such as a case for a sword). But we now know that there are openings in the myelin covering. They are called **nodes of Ranvier**, and they are the places where sodium ions can enter the cell. With a **myelinated** neuron, a signal can travel faster because it can skip from node to node; sodium ions do not need to enter at every channel. Also, myelinated neurons are less likely to be accidentally fired by the firing of a nearby neuron – they are more efficient. So, myelin is helpful; it allows cells to send signals faster and more efficiently. Newborn babies do not have much myelination. As they grow and develop, myelination will occur until reaching maturity around the age of 21 years. Unfortunately, there are a number of serious diseases that destroy myelin. **Multiple sclerosis** is the most common and well known of these.

Synaptic Transmission

Messages not only travel within neurons, but also travel between cells, from one neuron to another. In this case, the message is passed by a chemical process. The place where this chemical transfer occurs is called a **synapse**, and the process is called **synaptic transmission**. Scientists believe that the synapse is the key to the physiological processes of learning, memory, and other cognitive functions. It is estimated that a human brain contains nearly 500 trillion synapses. On average, each brain neuron communicates with about 1,000 other neurons through synapses.

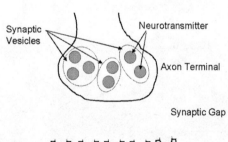

At the end of a neuron's axon are many branches called **terminals**. At the end of the terminals are enlarged regions called **buttons**. Inside the buttons are bags called **vesicles**. Inside the vesicles are chemical molecules known as **neurotransmitters** or just **transmitters**. When a neuron fires, those chemicals will be released and will transmit messages to other cells or to muscles.

When the inside of a terminal button becomes positively charged (when an action potential has reached the end of a neuron; when the neuron is depolarized), **calcium ions** enter the terminal button and cause some of the vesicles to open and to release their neurotransmitter chemicals. In other words, an action potential causes a neuron to squirt out a chemical. The transmitter chemical is squirted into the space between two neurons called the **synaptic gap** or **cleft**. The neurons do not touch each other; a chemical is released from the sending cell into the gap where it can bind with other, complementary chemicals on the receiving cell (the receptors).

The sending cell is called **presynaptic**, while the receiving cell is called **postsynaptic**. The neurotransmitter chemical passes from one neuron to the other. It is received by chemicals on the dendrites of the postsynaptic cell. The neurotransmitter chemical fits together with the receptors on the receiving dendrite. The process is usually likened to a key fitting into a lock: Each neurotransmitter fits into certain receptors. The neurotransmitter binds with the receptor.

When a neurotransmitter chemical binds with a receptor chemical on a receiving dendrite (when the key fits into the lock), a chemical reaction takes place. This causes the ion channels of the receiving cell to either open or to close. The transmitters that cause sodium ion channels to open are called **excitatory**, because they allow positively charged sodium ions to enter the neuron, causing depolarization and (maybe, if the threshold is reached!) an action potential. Some other transmitters are called **inhibitory**. They cause the cell to become less positively charged, thus making it more difficult to fire the neuron (they inhibit firing). It is necessary to have both types of neurotransmitters (excitatory and inhibitory), and to have them working in a proper balance. When we move an arm, for instance, we want some of our muscles to expand and some to contract. If all transmitters caused excitation, you would have an epileptic seizure every time you opened your eyes! We need both excitation and inhibition in proper balance.

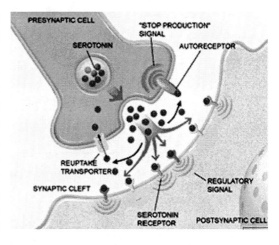

Curare is a poison used by South American indigenous people. It acts by blocking receptors used for muscle movement – an animal is paralyzed by inability to excite the muscles. On the other hand, some chemicals act by blocking the inhibitory chemicals. The poison **strychnine**, for instance, blocks the inhibition of muscle movements thus causing muscular convulsions and death.

Whether or not a postsynaptic (receiving) cell will fire depends upon the extent to which it receives excitatory and inhibitory neurotransmitter chemicals. This is a **more-or-less** process. Each neuron receives chemicals from many other cells, often thousands. It is the summation of these chemical messages that determines whether the cell will depolarize enough to fire. Imagine: A neuron will or will not fire based on the relative inputs of thousands of terminals squirting chemicals onto its dendrites. If the receiving neuron becomes positively charged enough to reach its threshold, then the cell will fire. By the way, synapses are changed by experience. That is, synapses can become easier to fire because of chemical and anatomical changes that occur. Brains are dynamic. They can change. That's right – you can learn!

Neurons act like little batteries changing electrical charge from negative to positive over and over again, each time squirting out a chemical transmitter that influences the micro-structure, biochemistry, and electrical firing of other neurons. The brain has billions of neurons, each making perhaps thousands of connections (synapses) with other cells. In essence, then, the brain is a biological, computational machine that transmits information both by electrical and chemical processes.

Clean-Up at the Synapse

After a neurotransmitter has been released by a neuron and is either in the synaptic gap or has been received by the receptors of another neuron, the whole mess must be cleaned up so that another message can come through. There are two ways that clean-up at the synapse occurs:

1. There are **enzymes** in the body that are housekeeping chemicals. Some of these enzymes have the job of recycling neurotransmitters; they attach to the neurotransmitter chemicals that have been released from the vesicles, and they recycle them. For example, one common enzyme that recycles transmitters is monoamine oxidase, commonly referred to as **MAO**. This enzyme is important for recycling the neurotransmitter **serotonin** and other neurotransmitters. Therefore, psychiatrists can use this fact to prescribe drugs that will influence the brain's enzymes. Treatment for depression is a good example.

People suffering from psychological depression often do not have enough serotonin activity in their brains. Today there are many drugs that can increase serotonin activity. The first of these, developed in the 1950s, is a class of drugs known as **MAO Inhibitors** or **MAOIs**. These drugs inhibit the enzyme MAO, thereby reducing the amount of serotonin that is recycled. The result is that there will be more serotonin in the synapse to stimulate the receptors. This helps many people with depression. One problem, however, is that people taking MAOIs must be warned not to eat certain foods or take certain medications because the combination could cause a heart attack. Since people are notoriously bad at following directions and will likely eat the foods that are forbidden, therefore MAOIs are not the first choice in treating depression today.

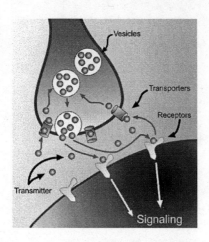

2. When a neurotransmitter is released by a neuron, some of the neurotransmitter molecules are carried back into the cell from which they came by molecules called **transporters**. That is, the presynaptic neuron, the sending neuron, squirts out a chemical and then some small amount of that chemical is brought back into the neuron. The squirt is followed by a suck! This process is called **reuptake**. Many drugs and medicines affect the transport of neurotransmitters back into the cell thus inhibiting the reuptake process. Cocaine, for example, is a drug that inhibits the reuptake of dopamine.

Some antidepressant medicines inhibit reuptake of serotonin, and sometimes inhibit reuptake of other neurotransmitters, too. The result is that less transmitter chemicals get pulled back into the presynaptic cell, leaving more transmitter chemicals in the gap to signal the receiving receptors. People with **depression** can take these medicines, **reuptake inhibitors**, to increase transmitter chemical activity in their brains. The best known of these drugs is **Prozac**, one of a group of drugs known as **selective serotonin reuptake inhibitors** (**SSRIs**). Others in this group include Paxil, Zoloft, and Celexa. The SSRIs work by decreasing the reuptake of serotonin, thereby allowing more serotonin to cross to the postsynaptic cell. Some other antidepressants are reuptake inhibitors for other neurotransmitters. These medicines include Wellbutrin, Cymbalta, Pristiq, and Effexor. For many people, these drugs improve mood, reduce anxiety, or help with compulsive or addictive behaviors by increasing the activity of various neurotransmitters in brain pathways.

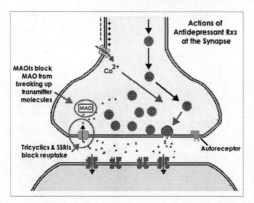

Neurotransmitters

There are many different neurotransmitters; about a hundred have been identified. One of the most common neurotransmitters in the brain is **acetylcholine**. This chemical is used in many pathways of the brain and body, and therefore influences many behaviors and mental states. For example, muscle movements depend on acetylcholine, but so do memories and thoughts. Sensory functions, arousal, attention, reward, and sleep all depend to some extent on acetylcholine.

People with **Alzheimer's disease** have decreased levels of acetylcholine. Sometimes medicine can improve cognitive processes in patients with Alzheimer's. Drugs such as Aricept, Exelon, and Reminyl can improve cognition by slowing the breakdown of acetylcholine. Though the results are only modest and temporary, such medicines are effective because they increase the amount of acetylcholine in the brain and therefore help cognitive processes, such as memory. Unfortunately, side effects, such as liver damage, may occur because acetylcholine is active in parts of the body other than the brain.

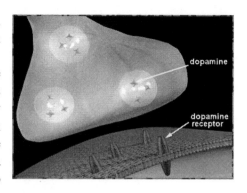

Another important neurotransmitter is **dopamine**. Dopamine is found in a number of brain pathways and therefore influences many psychological qualities, including mood, thinking, and body movement. In **Parkinson's disease**, the brain cannot make enough dopamine. The brain region that manufactures this chemical (the **substantia nigra**) has been damaged. The damage can occur in a number of ways; heredity is sometimes involved, and exposure to toxins, such as pesticides and herbicides, is often a cause.

Both Alzheimer's and Parkinson's occur more often in older people. Alzheimer's patients show cognitive problems, such as memory impairment. The first symptoms of Parkinson's are tremor, uncontrollable shaking (particularly of the hands in the early stages) and other muscle movement problems. Patients with Parkinson's can take a medicine, such as **L-dopa**, that is a precursor of dopamine that helps the brain make more dopamine. This will work for a while, but eventually the brain will become so damaged that it cannot make dopamine even with the precursor chemical.

Today there are no cures for Alzheimer's or Parkinson's, but electrodes placed into the brain, surgery, and brain cell transplants are having some limited success in relieving symptoms. In one case, adult stem cells were removed from a patient's brain, they were grown into neurons in the laboratory, then were implanted back into the brain. The patient's Parkinsonian tremors largely disappeared (Levesque, 2002). We can hope that science will uncover effective cures for these serious diseases in the near future.

When L-dopa was first used in treating Parkinson's, it was discovered that patients who took too much of the medicine began to show symptoms similar to those of the severe psychotic disorder **schizophrenia**. Contrary to popular belief, this disorder is not the same as split personality; but, rather is a serious brain disorder that causes people to have hallucinations, delusions, and abnormal thinking. Since Parkinson's disease patients exhibited these symptoms when they took excessive amounts of L-dopa, scientists theorized that schizophrenia was linked to excess dopamine. This view became known as the **dopamine hypothesis**. Scientists guessed that people with schizophrenia might have excessive amounts of dopamine receptors. This proved to be correct for many people with schizophrenia.

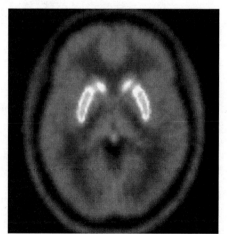

Higher levels of dopamine activity are found in the brains of people with schizophrenia and those at risk of developing psychosis.

An excess of receptors could come about from genetic factors, or maybe exposure to viruses prenatally. Medicines used to treat schizophrenia work by blocking dopamine receptors. These drugs are called **neuroleptic** (literally, "grasping the neuron") or **antipsychotic** drugs. These medicines help reduce symptoms in about 80% of patients with schizophrenia. Unfortunately, long-term use of neuroleptic drugs can cause impairment in the dopamine system. The result is **tardive dyskinesia**, a disorder in which patients have uncontrollable muscle twitches, similar to Parkinson's disease. There are a number of new medicines, called atypical (or second generation) neuroleptics, that act more narrowly on various dopamine receptors, and hence are more effective for some patients.

Serotonin (also known as 5-HT), mentioned above, is a very common neurotransmitter found in many different pathways in the brain. It's a bit like electricity

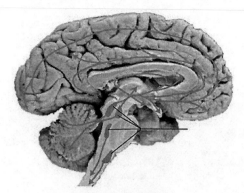

Serotonin pathways.

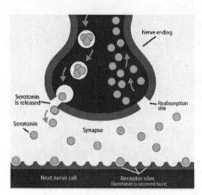

Serotonin synapse.

in your house: used for lots of purposes. Both dopamine and serotonin are released by a small number of neurons in the brain, but they make thousands of connections; so, these two transmitters are involved in many functions. While serotonin is typically linked to depression, in fact the chemical plays various roles in mind and behavior. It is not a good idea to try to match neurotransmitters with certain psychological processes. Brains are complex biological organs whose properties and processes do not line up neatly with our English language concepts!

The chemicals used for communication in the brain are found in many different brain areas, and are found in the body proper, also. For example, serotonin is found in the gut where it regulates intestinal functions, in the blood as a vasoconstrictor, and also as a brain neurotransmitter is involved with mood, appetite, evaluating social situations, sleep, learning, and anxiety. There are many drugs and medicines that can increase serotonin. Antidepressants are generally safe, however, there is some risk of a serious side effect known as **serotonin syndrome**, which can occur with the use of any substances that increase serotonin activity.

Glutamate is the most common excitatory chemical in the brain and is intimately involved in learning, memory, and cognitive processes. People suffering from schizophrenia and other psychological disorders often have impairments in their glutamate systems. The result is cognitive impairments of various kinds involving memory, thinking, making decisions, etc. One of the glutamate receptors, known as **NMDA**, has been intensely studied because of its role in plasticity at the synapse, learning, and memory.

Another important neurotransmitter is **GABA**. Because GABA is an inhibitory chemical, it slows or inhibits the firing of neurons. When GABA receptors are stimulated, we feel relaxed, calmed, and slowed-down. The receptors for GABA also respond to alcohol. So, one effect of alcohol is to inhibit the nervous system, to slow reflex reactions, to relax muscles. GABA receptors also are influenced by certain medicines known as **antianxiety drugs**. Benzodiazepines, such as Xanax, are one type of antianxiety drug. They stimulate GABA receptors and calm the nervous system. It is important not to mix antianxiety pills with alcohol because the combined effect on the GABA receptors could slow the nervous system to the point of death. Such deaths have occurred both accidentally and intentionally.

Finally, a common neurotransmitter is **norepinephrine**, which is also a hormone. Norepinephrine is implicated in depression, mania, anxiety, stress, the fight or flight response, and body regulation of heart rate and blood pressure. Many different brain regions use this important chemical as a neurotransmitter. Along with dopamine, norepinephrine plays a role in **attention deficit/hyperactivity disorder** (ADHD). One class of antidepressant drugs (SNRI) inhibits the reuptake of this transmitter, and therefore is useful in treating a number of psychological disorders.

Mimicry

Psychoactive drugs pass the blood-brain barrier and alter brain functioning. Such substances affect us psychologically because they influence chemical processes in the brain that regulate emotion, mood, thinking, and perceiving. Many psychoactive drugs act physiologically because they mimic natural neurotransmitters. Heroin, LSD, and marijuana are **agonists** that stimulate receptors that are normally stimulated by natural chemicals the brain uses at the synapses in various brain regions. The hallucinogen LSD has numerous effects on the brain, one of which is that it acts as an agonist for the neurotransmitter serotonin. Heroin mimics brain transmitters known as **endorphins** (literally: internal morphine) that naturally aid pain relief and give a sense of well-being. Marijuana's active ingredient, THC, found in cannabis, is an agonist. The cannabis molecule has a shape similar to natural neurotransmitters known as **endocannabinoids** (literally: inside, similar to cannabis). One of the endocannabinoids is the transmitter **anandamide**, which is involved in learning, pain relief, mood, desire, appetite (cannabis gives one "the munchies"), and memory (long-term marijuana use causes memory difficulty).

Most psychoactive drugs are agonists that mimic natural neurotransmitters. **Cocaine**, however, is not an agonist, but works primarily as a reuptake inhibitor for dopamine in the reward pathway of the brain. This means that cocaine has the effect of increasing the amount of dopamine activity in that brain region (less dopamine is transported back into the sending cell), leading to a euphoric effect.

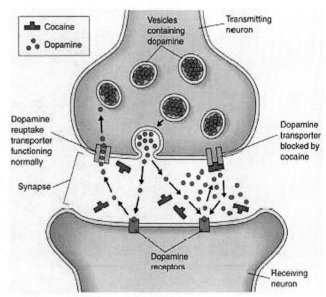

There are also drugs known as **antagonists** that act against natural transmitters. Sometimes antagonists are laboratory-produced medicines used to treat mental disorders. Neuroleptic (antipsychotic) drugs, mentioned above, that are used to treat psychotic disorders such as schizophrenia, are antagonists primarily for dopamine – they block dopamine receptors.

Understanding how neurons work is important not only for scientists who want to find cures for disorders, but also in helping to explain the mind and behavior. There undoubtedly will arise more fascinating and startling discoveries as scientists reveal even more about the intricate workings of neurons, the beautiful butterflies of our souls.

Cocaine increases dopamine activity in the pleasure pathway of the brain by inhibiting the reuptake of dopamine at the synapse.

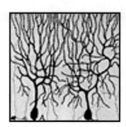

Chapter 6

SPLIT BRAIN
Two brains are better than one!

The nervous system is a communication system. It communicates messages throughout the body. The cells of the nervous system receive and send messages. These messages are received from stimuli outside of the body (coming from the surroundings, such as light, sound, and tastes), and from within the body (coming from other neurons). The signals are directed toward the brain, where they are processed, or to various parts of the body, such as the endocrine system, the muscles, or the body organs. The nervous system communicates by receiving and sending signals. This communication system is divided into various components.

Divisions

The brain and the spinal cord together are known as the **central nervous system (CNS)** because that is where all signals either go to or come from. The brain and spinal cord are at the center of the communications.

The nerves that bring messages from the body to the spinal cord, together with the nerves that send messages out from the spinal cord to the body proper, make up the **peripheral nervous system (PNS)**. These nerves are further divided into two categories: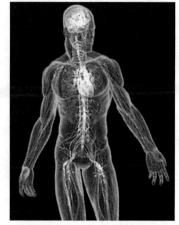

1. The **somatic nervous system (SNS)** consists of nerves that bring in messages about sensations (the **senses**), and the nerves that go to the skeletal muscles that move us around (the **motor nerves**). The SNS often operates under our conscious control. We are able to see, hear, and move about in our environment because of this system of nerves.

2. The **autonomic nervous system (ANS)** works mostly automatically in the control of body organs and basic life functions. When

you go jogging, you don't need to remember to beat your heart faster; your ANS will take care of that. When you hear a sudden, very loud noise, you don't need to remember to be startled; your ANS will do it automatically. When you are nervous, the nerves of your ANS will make you breathe harder to get more oxygen into your lungs. After you've eaten a big meal, don't concern yourself with remembering to digest the food, because your ANS is on the job.

The ANS works automatically, however, it does interact with the SNS to some degree, and therefore the ANS can be affected somewhat by conscious thought. On average, we have about 10% control over the ANS functions of our bodies. For example, you can change your heartbeat, your blood pressure, and other autonomic functions by about 10% by using conscious control, by thinking. Some people are much better at this than others, of course, and this control can be developed to some extent through practice. Still, the ANS mostly functions automatically.

The ANS is further divided into two divisions: a) the **sympathetic division** is made up of the nerves that use up energy when in situations of activation, such as danger. These nerves speed up your heart, increase your blood pressure, release adrenalin, and so on. b) The **parasympathetic division** consists of nerves that do just the opposite. This set of nerves slows you down, relaxes you, and helps you conserve energy by digesting food, and reducing heartbeat and blood pressure. These two systems work together (automatically, without conscious thought) in keeping our bodies working smoothly.

Cerebrum

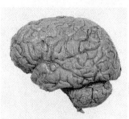

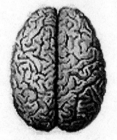

When one looks at a brain, probably the first thing that is noticed is the wrinkly part on the top, the **cerebrum**. This part of the brain is responsible for higher mental functions, purposeful body movement, memory, and executive thinking. The cerebrum is very large in humans, but a much smaller percentage of lower animals's brains, although the chimpanzee cerebrum is very similar to that of a human. The human cerebrum, if removed from the head and ironed, would be about as large as a table top and very thin. Imagine a large piece of paper that must be crumpled to fit inside a smaller sphere. One can get an estimate of the size of an animal's cerebrum by looking at how many wrinkles it has.

The wrinkles on the cerebrum are called **fissures** or **sulci** (singular = **sulcus**). The bumps that are formed by the wrinkling of the cerebrum are called **gyri** (singular = **gyrus**). These anatomical features are used as geographic boundaries for labeling parts of the brain. If you looked at a brain from the top, you would see that the cerebrum is divided from front to back by what is called the **longitudinal fissure**. This groove divides the cerebrum into left and right sides known as **hemispheres**. Don't take the term literally ("half-spheres"), since

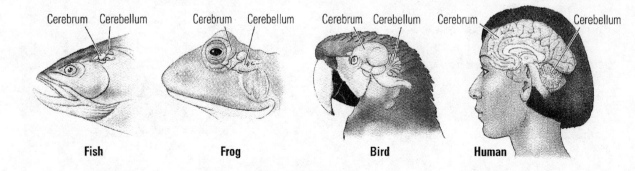

| Cerebrum   Cerebellum | Cerebrum   Cerebellum | Cerebrum   Cerebellum | Cerebrum   Cerebellum |

Fish   **Frog**   **Bird**   **Human**

the cerebrum is not shaped like a sphere – it is more ovoid in form. Differences between the left and right hemispheres have been studied extensively, and this chapter will delineate the major findings.

Two Highways

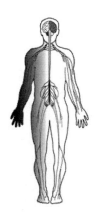

With only a few exceptions, the brain's left hemisphere is connected to the right side of the body and the right hemisphere is connected to the left side of the body. This connection is called **contralateral**, meaning "opposite sides." If a person has a stroke or other damage in the left hemisphere, the disability will be on the right side of his body. Similarly, damage in the right hemisphere will result in problems on the left side of the body. Also, if you touch something with your left hand, the signal is sent to the right hemisphere of your brain. And, too, if you want to move your right hand, the signal must originate in the left hemisphere of your cerebrum. The brain and body are wired left to right and right to left.

The **spinal cord** is a series of thin cables (**nerves**) traveling up and down the back protected by the vertebral column. The spinal cord carries signals to and from the brain and the body. These signals are transmitted only in one direction; they are not two-way highways. Some of the spinal cord nerves carry signals from the body to the brain, for example when you touch something with your hand. If these signals are damaged, or if the part of the brain that processes these signals is damaged, then you will experience **numbness**, a lack of feeling in your body.

Other nerves in the spinal cord carry signals away from your brain to the muscles of your skeleton (so you can move). These signals travel from the brain down the spinal cord and then to muscles in various parts of the body. If these nerves are damaged, or if the part of the brain that originates these signals is damaged, then you will experience **paralysis**. Please note that numbness and paralysis are *not* at all the same thing; they are different conditions that are caused by damage to different systems of brain and nerves.

The crossover points for the contralateral wiring of the nervous system are in the spinal cord or the brainstem, depending on which nerves are involved. For example, if you touch something with your *right* hand, an electrical signal travels up your right arm to your spinal cord, then crosses over to the *left* side of the spinal cord, and then travels up to the *left hemisphere*. Therefore your left hemisphere feels something touching your right hand. Similarly, motor signals coming from the left hemisphere cross over and go to the right side of the body. To move your right hand requires an electrical signal originating in the left hemisphere.

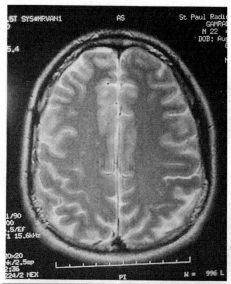

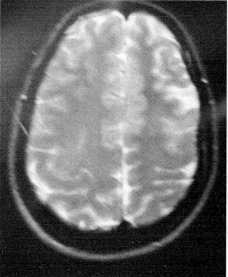

The top image shows the hemispheres of a normal brain. The bottom image is a brain in which the right hemisphere is smaller, probably the result of fetal alcohol syndrome. The woman complained of numbness and weakness on the left side of her body.

So, in effect, we have two highway systems of nerves: One set of nerves (known as the **afferent** or **sensory nerves**) carries signals from the body's parts to the spinal cord and brain, giving us the sense of touch and feeling in our body. Another set or nerves (known as the **efferent** or **motor nerves**) carries signals away from the brain and spinal cord to our body's parts, giving us movement of our skeletal muscles.

The above facts refer to the nerves that extend up and down the spinal cord connecting brain and body proper. There also are **cranial nerves**: 12 pairs of nerves that serve sensation and movement in the head ("cranium" means the skull), particularly in the face. Not all of the cranial nerves are contralateral, some are **ipsilateral** ("same side"), and sometimes they consist of fibers that carry signals in two directions, thus conveying both skin sensations and muscle movement in the face. As information travels through various areas of the brain, the pathways are known as **tracts**. For example, one would speak of the optic tract that carries signals from the optic nerves to various parts of the brain.

The Hard Body

Now, if you think about the connections and highways of nerves described above, you will realize that there must be some means by which the left and right hemispheres communicate with each other. We do not have two independent hemispheres; we have a system of coordination – one brain. The communication between hemispheres is accomplished by a bundle of fibers that carries information from the left hemisphere to the right and from the right to the left.

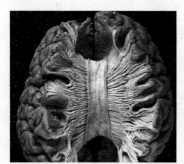
The corpus callosum seen from below.

Deep down inside the cerebrum there is an area of connection called the **corpus callosum**. This term literally means a "hard body." If you had a brain in your hand and you pushed your fingers down between the two hemispheres – in the longitudinal fissure – you would eventually (after an inch or two) feel the corpus callosum. This is the brain part (the tract) that sends signals back and forth between the two hemispheres so that one hemisphere can "know" what the other "knows." The corpus callosum is the communication tract between the left and right hemispheres.

Amazingly, there are some instances in which a person's corpus callosum is cut by surgeons. This is done in rare cases of severe **epilepsy** so to save a person's life. Epilepsy is the condition in which a person has repetitive **seizures**, abnormal electrical firings of brain cells. These are like short circuits occurring within the brain. Epilepsy is fairly common and could affect anyone, although it is more common among children. There are many causes of epilepsy, including genetic factors, birth problems, diseases, infections, and brain trauma. Sometimes epilepsy is mild, and there are few discernible problems associated with the seizures. Sometimes the seizures are more severe and more difficult to control. Most people with epilepsy take medication to control their seizures. In the most severe cases, the abnormal electrical activity can cross over the corpus callosum from one hemisphere to the other and the person could die. In these rare cases, a surgical operation is performed to cut the corpus callosum.

The operation that is done could be called a corpus callosotomy, but it is more commonly called **split-brain surgery**. Don't be confused by the terminology, this has nothing to do with split personality, a psychological disorder known as dissociative identity disorder. Split brain patients do not have this disorder. In split-brain surgery, surgeons sever the fibers that carry signals between the left and right hemispheres, the corpus callosum. The result is that the two hemispheres of the cerebrum then are separated and act independently

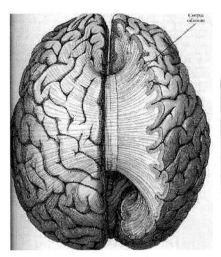
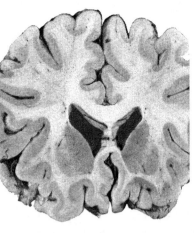
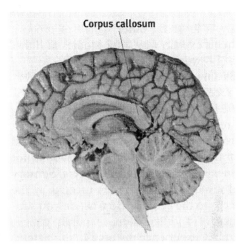

Corpus callosum

Three views of the corpus callosum.

of one another; they are unable to receive signals from each other. The person who has had split-brain surgery, in effect, has two half brains that cannot talk to each other. Nothing whatsoever changes about the patient's personality, abilities, knowledge, memories, senses, or intelligence. The split brain patient is the same person after the surgery as they were before. However, the left and right hemispheres of the cerebrum cannot send signals to one another. What must that feel like?

To the Side

The study of split-brain patients has confirmed that certain behaviors and psychological functions are processed more in one hemisphere than the other. In these cases, the behavior or function is said to be **lateralized** (meaning "to the side"). If we say that a particular function is lateralized, we mean that one hemisphere is better than the other at performing or processing that function.

For example, though a small percentage of people process language in their right hemispheres, and an even smaller percentage use both hemispheres for language, in the vast majority of people language is lateralized to the left. (It's easy to remember: **L**anguage is in the **L**eft hemisphere). The cerebrum's right hemisphere (in nearly everyone) does not understand and create language. For most of us, in order to use grammar, syntax, semantics, sentence structure, and proper pronunciation, it is necessary to have a normally functioning left hemisphere. In fact, we can see a bump in the left hemisphere that is not present on the right in the vast majority of brains.

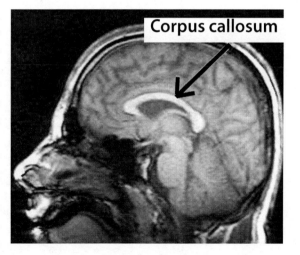

Corpus callosum

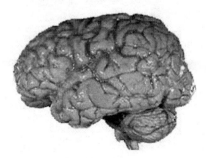

Left hemisphere.

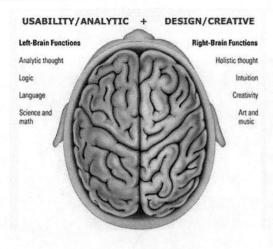

USABILITY/ANALYTIC + DESIGN/CREATIVE

Left-Brain Functions	Right-Brain Functions
Analytic thought	Holistic thought
Logic	Intuition
Language	Creativity
Science and math	Art and music

While the left hemisphere is especially good at processing language, the right hemisphere specializes in spatial perception, or **visuospatial** processes (being able to mentally picture things in space, such as a map of your surroundings, orienting in space, or locating objects in the environment). The differences between the hemispheres are not based on the nature of the stimuli we sense, but on the type of cognitive operation the brain must do to interpret our world (Stephan, 2003). For instance, understanding what a word means is more a left hemisphere task, while understanding where that word is on a page is more a right hemisphere task.

Left hemispheres deal more in details, logic, language, and analysis. Right hemispheres excel at maps, musical melodies, visual orientation, patterns, and whole forms. To the left hemisphere, for example, the sound of one saxophone is about the same as a second saxophone; a face is made of nose, mouth, eyes, etc. But, to the right hemisphere, a particular saxophone has a specific pattern or whole form that is different from other saxophones. And, a face is a unique pattern of parts, not just an accumulation of parts. The left hemisphere is concerned with the parts, the details; the right hemisphere, on the contrary, specializes in finding the whole pattern, the form.

The differences between the hemispheres have led many people to devise wild ideas about left- and right-brained people. This is not a good idea. We have a corpus callosum that shares information between the hemispheres. Our right and left hemispheres communicate with each other. Yes, it's true that some people are better at some skills and psychological functions than are other people, but for the vast majority of mental functions, we are all two-hemisphere people! We do not have half a brain or even two brains. We have two halves that work together.

The differences between the two hemispheres are mostly a matter of degree – one hemisphere does something a little better than the other. A good example is the brain's processing of music. Textbooks for years have stated that this is a right hemisphere function. But one study used brain imaging to show that some music interpretation is computed in the area of the left hemisphere that processes grammar (Maess, 2001). In fact, an accomplished musician who reads music is more likely to use the left hemisphere when listening to a concert, while those of us who only listen to the melody are using our right hemispheres. It is better to think of the brain as a tightly organized bundle of interacting modules than to divide it into clearly distinct regions with their own completely separate functions. After all, a brain is a communicating machine, and it's various complex regions are highly interconnected.

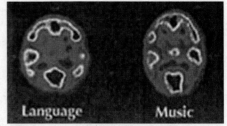

Slightly more activity on the left in response to language; and a bit more on the right when hearing music.

Handedness

As is quite obvious, some people are better at writing with their right hand, and some are better with their left, and a very small number are equally good with right and left (are ambidextrous). Check the lengths of your thumbs right now. Go ahead, put them next to each other. Is one longer than the other? Is the thumb on your preferred hand longer? I thought so! Is it wider, too?

Scientists do not know exactly what causes handedness, but there seem to be many variables involved, including some genetic factors and some environmental. There has always been pressure from culture for children to be right-handed, for example. Though a gene was been found in 1998 that strongly influences left-handedness, inheritance is not the sole cause. Two left-handed parents have only a 26% chance of having a left-handed child. Identical twins have a concordance rate of 76% for handedness. And, handedness for writing does not carry over to left/right hemisphere abilities, nor to other parts of the body. Which hand a person uses when writing or doing fine motor skills has little to do with overall brain architecture – it has to do with which hemisphere does a better, more controlled job of handling a pencil. A person who writes with the right hand may kick with the left foot. How about you? I suspect you can find some things you do better with the left side of the body, and some better with the right.

Some stone-age tools are left-handed, but the vast majority are right-handed, showing that this difference has been around for a long time.

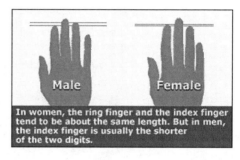

In women, the ring finger and the index finger tend to be about the same length. But in men, the index finger is usually the shorter of the two digits.

About 10% of people are left handed and 90% are right handed. The percentage of left-handers is higher in men than in women, probably because prenatal testosterone (more in men) slows left hemisphere development and increases right hemisphere development. Women, on the average, excel at verbal skills (left hemisphere tasks), while men excel at spatial perception, a right hemisphere ability. Left-handed students are more likely to major in visually-based, as opposed to language-based subjects, and a large percentage of art students are left handed or ambidextrous (Bragdon & Gamon, 2001); this may be related to prenatal development of the right hemisphere. Females who had a male DZ twin score higher on mental rotation tests because of their prenatal exposure to testosterone (Vuoksimaa, 2010). Finger length is influenced by

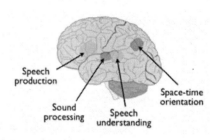

Speech production

Sound processing

Speech understanding

Space-time orientation

prenatal testosterone, too. If your index finger is longer than your ring finger, this suggests good verbal ability. However, if your index finger is shorter than your ring finger it means there was more prenatal testosterone, which means good spatial perception. Which one are you? Most people have longer fingers on their dominant hand, by the way.

Language in the brain is only partly related to handedness. About half of left-handers have language control in the left hemisphere, while about 95% of right-handers have language in the left hemisphere. About one-fourth of lefties process language in both hemispheres. So, we can see, language is strongly lateralized in the left hemisphere.

It is often said that a disproportional percentage of geniuses are left handed. This is true. However, it is also true that a disproportionate number of people who are intellectually delayed are left handed! How could that be? One reason for this seemingly incongruous fact is that left-handers have a wider distribution statistically than do right-handers. If we look at people in the middle of intelligence, we will find slightly more than 90% right-handers, while at the extremes – high or low – there will be slightly fewer than 90% right handed, while slightly more than ten percent will be left handed. Left-handers vary more in most traits, so there will be proportionately more left-handers than expected in the extremes of many different characteristics. In some cases, however, the gene involved in left-handedness, or the hormones present prenatally that contribute to left-handedness, may also have contributed to some psychological characteristics, such as autism, intellectual disability, or schizophrenia. These are only partial influences, however.

Since handedness refers to handwriting, it is not unusual for people to use one hand or the other for different tasks. A right-hander might swing a bat left handed, for example. Such mixed dominance is quite common. The dominant eye is usually on the same side as the dominant hand, but not always. You can check which of your eyes is dominant by pointing at something far away and then checking to see which eye you are using by closing each eye while your arm and finger hold their pointing position. Which of your eyes is dominant?

Animals show a preference for one hand when using tools (Hopkins, 2007). A look at the brain areas being used shows that chimpanzees use areas that are similar to the language areas found in human brains. This indicates that the brain areas for tool use may have served as preparation for the evolution of language. Do you speak with your hands? Perhaps the human brain speech areas evolved out of our early ancestors' brain areas for use of tools.

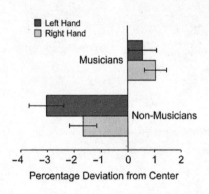

Now try this: Draw a horizontal line on a piece of paper. Go ahead, I'll wait. Draw a horizontal line. Did you do it? Now, just by looking at the line, make a mark where you think the exact middle of the line is. Mark the center. Did you do it? Now get a ruler and measure the line to see where the exact middle is. I'll wait again. Hmmm. Hmmm. Hmmm. Okay, are you done? I'll bet your guess about the center is a little bit to the left of the true center. This is called **pseudoneglect** and researchers believe it results from the fact that your right hemisphere is in charge of visuospatial tasks and neglects the right field of vision a little bit (Hausmann, 2002). Right-handers will experience this more than lefties. Interestingly, musicians are more accurate at judging the center of a horizontal line (Patston, 2006). Perhaps it's because musical training enhances visuospatial perception.

By the way, patients with brain damage, particularly if it is in the right hemisphere, sometimes show the odd perception of not noticing objects or people in their left field of vision, a condition known as **hemispatial neglect**. Such a patient may be asked to copy a drawing, but the copy they make will be of only the right half. The left side is neglected, as if it is not there. But, if it is pointed out, the patient does notice it.

Split Brain Findings

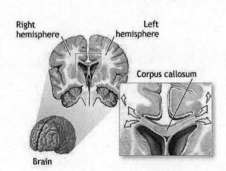

As mentioned above, split-brain patients have been studied extensively. If a person's corpus callosum has been cut, then signals cannot be sent from one cerebral hemisphere to the other; the left and right hemispheres are isolated from one another. This means that whatever information is processed in one hemisphere cannot be shared with the other hemisphere.

For example, suppose we blindfold a split-brain patient and then place an object, say a pencil, into her left hand. Her left hand touches the pencil and sends a signal about the pencil to her spinal cord where the signal ascends upward to her right cerebral hemisphere, to the part of the brain that processes the feeling of the pencil. We might say that her right hemisphere "knows" about the pencil; it feels it and remembers it. The right hemisphere, however, cannot send a message over to the left hemisphere because the corpus callosum has been severed. So the left hemisphere "knows" nothing about the pencil; it cannot receive any information about it, not from the left hand and not from the right hemisphere. If we then take the pencil from her left hand and place it on a table with a number of other objects and ask her to find it with her right hand (which is guided by the left hemisphere, which did not feel the pencil), she cannot identify the pencil as the object she was just holding; that is, her left hemisphere cannot identify the pencil. However, if she uses her left hand to find the pencil, she can do it because the left hand receives signals from the right hemisphere, which felt the pencil.

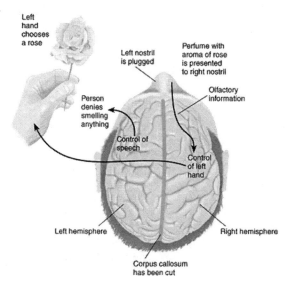

We might ask if the split-brain patient knows about the pencil or if she can feel the pencil. The answer is an astounding one: Her right hemisphere can feel the pencil and so it knows about the pencil, but her left hemisphere does not. She now has a right mind and a left mind; she is two people, in a certain way. Her brain cannot share information from one cerebral hemisphere to the other, so what one hemisphere knows is separated from what the other knows.

Next we put a pencil in her left hand and ask the split-brain patient to *tell* us what she is holding. Remember, the signal from the left hand travels to the right hemisphere, which does not control language. The left hemisphere controls language, so it will do the speaking. But it does not know about the pencil; it cannot receive information from the right hemisphere or from the left hand. Therefore, the left hemisphere will honestly say, "I do not know." The split-brain patient says she does not know what she is holding in her left hand! Her left hemisphere is speaking and telling the truth; it really doesn't know. But, you might wonder, does she know? Well, again, there are two minds here. Although her left hemisphere does not know about the pencil, her right hemisphere does. How can we be sure? We can ask her to find the pencil among a group of objects using her left hand. She can do that. Also, we could ask her to draw a picture of the object using her left hand. She can do that. Any task that asks the question of the right hemisphere will give us the answer. Her right hemisphere knows, but her left does not.

By the way, in the examples above we are asking the patient to respond; that means she is using her hearing, her auditory sense. How is that wired in the brain? When we ask a question or give directions to the patient, both hemispheres receive the auditory message. Each ear is connected to both brain hemispheres; however, a bit more of the message from an ear goes to the opposite hemisphere than to the same-side hemisphere.

Split Vision

But what about vision? What happens if a split brain patient looks at an object? There are cells in the very back of the eyes that are sensitive to light. These cells send signals to the occipital lobe in the very back of the cerebrum via the **optic nerve**. There are two optic nerves, one coming out of the back of each eye. The two optic nerves meet half-way back in the brain at a junction called the **optic chiasm**. At that point, the nerves divide, sending information from cells on the left to the left hemisphere and information from cells on

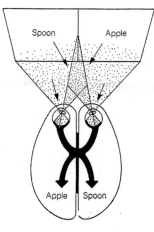

the right to the right hemisphere. The visual information is routed to the visual processing areas in the occipital lobes in the back of the cerebrum. In most of us, the two hemispheres then share the information they received with each other. However, a split-brain patient has no corpus callosum with which to share visual information.

Dog

Fixation Point

The way the eyes are wired to the brain is very interesting. The cells on the left side *of each eye* are wired to the *left* hemisphere, while the cells on the right side *of each eye* are connected to the *right* hemisphere. Now, think about this: Cells on the left side of either eye are wired to the left hemisphere, while cells on the right side of either eye are wired to the right hemisphere. Cells on the left, go to the left. Cells on the right, go to the right. That means we see objects that are on the left in our right hemispheres, and we see objects on the right in our left hemispheres.

Each eye sends signals to both the left and right hemispheres. The cells on the left (inside, very back) of the eye send their signals to the left hemisphere, while the cells on the right of the eye send their signals to the right hemisphere. However, cells on the right side of the eye receive light from objects on the left, while cells on the left of the eye receive light from objects in the right field of vision. Each eye sends signals to both hemispheres. The cells of the eye that respond to light are in the very back inside of the eye in a layer known as the **retina**. The cells on the left of the retina respond to objects in the right visual field, and are wired to the left hemisphere. This is true for both eyes. So, both eyes send signals to the left hemisphere about objects that are on the right. Similarly, retinal cells on the right side of each eye receive light from objects in the left visual field and are wired to the right hemisphere of the brain.

Because of the way the eyes are wired to the hemispheres of the brain, the result is that we see things that are on the *left* in our *right* hemisphere, and we see things that are on our *right* in our *left* hemisphere. If an object is in your *left* field of vision, then the light coming from it will strike the cells on the *right* side of the back of each eye. Thus, an

Testing a split-brain patient: An image on the left side of the screen is seen by the right hemisphere which can identify the object using the left hand. But the left hemisphere did not see the image, so cannot say what it is. The left hemisphere sees only what is on the right - in this case, nothing.

object in your left visual field stimulates cells on the right side of the back of each eye. And, those cells on the right side of each eye are connected to the right hemisphere. Therefore, an object on the left will be seen in the right hemisphere. Likewise, an object in the *right* visual field will stimulate cells on the *left* side of each eye, cells that are wired to the left hemisphere. So, the left hemisphere sees things on the right while the right hemisphere sees things on the left.

Okay, now suppose a split-brain patient sits in front of a screen and is shown pictures projected on the left and on the right sides of the screen. Pictures on the right will be processed by her left hemisphere, while pictures on the left will be processed by her right hemisphere. Unlike in us, her corpus callosum has been cut, so the hemispheres cannot share information with each other.

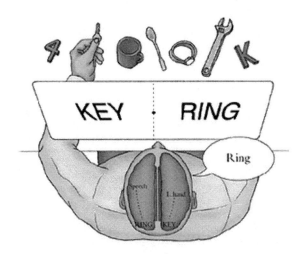

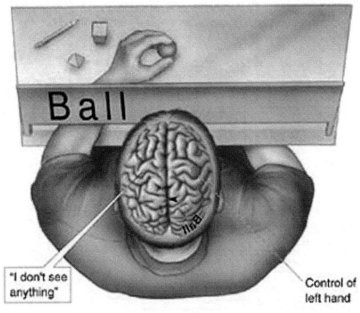

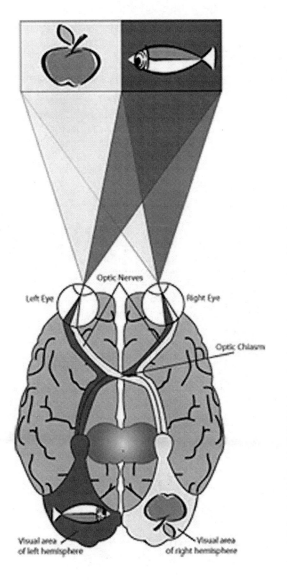

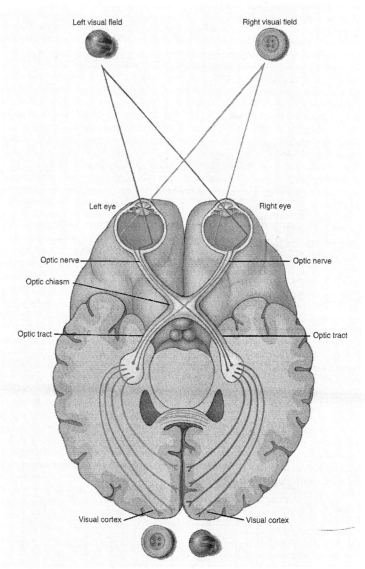

For a split-brain patient, the left hemisphere sees a man while the right hemisphere sees a woman. What will patients say they saw? A man. Because left hemispheres control language.

If we put a picture of a ball on the left side of the screen and a picture of a dog on the right side of the screen, her brain will see the ball in the right hemisphere and the dog in the left hemisphere. If we then give her a group of pictures and ask her to point to the object she saw using her left hand, she will point to a picture of a ball (left hand is controlled by right hemisphere, which sees things on the left). However, if we ask her to tell us what she saw, she will say "dog" since the left hemisphere controls speaking and it sees things on the right. Her left hand points at a ball, but she says "dog."

One woman who had split-brain surgery was found to have *spoken* language controlled by her left hemisphere, but *written* language was controlled in her right hemisphere. Words flashed to her left hemisphere could be spoken, but not written, while words flashed to her right hemisphere could be written, but not spoken. So, at least in some people, these two functions of language are found in different hemispheres (Baynes, 1998).

If we place an object in the patient's right field of vision, then it is seen by the left hemisphere and the person can say what it is. However, she will not be able to identify it with her left hand, since that hand is controlled by the right hemisphere. On the other hand (pun intended), if we put an object in the left visual field of the patient, then her right hemisphere will see it. In that case, she will not be able to talk about it, but she will be able to identify it with her left hand. When we see objects in our left field of vision, the visual signal is processed in the right hemisphere; objects in our right field of vision are processed in the left hemisphere. Of course for most of us, the information can pass via the corpus callosum to the opposite hemisphere for further processing. The split-brain patient cannot share information between hemispheres.

The Interpreting Brain

In a well-known case study, a split-brain patient was shown a snowy scene on the left (seen by her right hemisphere) and a chicken claw on the right (seen by her left hemisphere). Then the patient was asked to point to pictures that corresponded with what she had seen. Her left hand (controlled by the right hemisphere) pointed to a shovel, and her right hand (controlled by the left hemisphere) pointed to a chicken. When asked why she was pointing to these things (remember, the left hemisphere does the speaking), she said she was pointing to the chicken because she saw a chicken claw, and she was pointing to the shovel because you use a shovel to clean out a chicken shed! The left hemisphere saw the chicken and did not know why the left hand (controlled by the right hemisphere that saw the snowy scene on the left) was pointing at a shovel. So, the left hemisphere interpreted the behavior by reaching a conclusion that seemed reasonable and plausible.

What this shows us is that humans give explanations. Apparently, we like to have reasons for what we do. The process is called **confabulation**. Perhaps it is learned, or perhaps it is a part of our evolutionary development, this tendency, this disposition to explain our behavior, to confabulate. Whatever the cause, we do it automatically, without being aware that we are doing it. The split-brain patient believes her explanation; she is not telling a lie.

Confabulation has been studied extensively by Michael Gazzaniga, who has written a number of books and articles about the differences between the right and left hemispheres. Working with a split-brain patient, Gazzaniga showed the patient's right hemisphere the word "laugh" and the patient began to laugh. When asked why he was laughing, he said, "You guys come up and test us every month. What a way to make a living!" When the word "walk" was shown to the split-brain patient's right

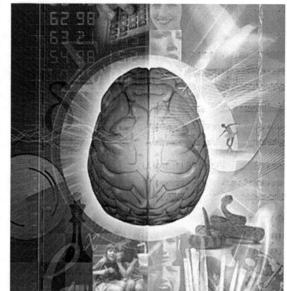

hemisphere, he got up to leave. When he was asked where he was going, he confabulated, "I'm thirsty, I'm going to get a Coke." That's the patient's left hemisphere talking; it confabulates a reason to explain his behavior. We know that the cause of the behavior is the word shown to the right hemisphere. But because the patient's corpus callosum has been cut, the left hemisphere does not know about the word, it cannot receive information from the right hemisphere, and it simply confabulates a reason for the observed behavior.

In each case the patient's left hemisphere shows all indications that it believes the explanations it has made up. Our left hemispheres apparently have a tendency to interpret or explain behaviors. Apparently we all do it; well, that is, our left hemispheres, the language hemispheres, do it. We make up good-sounding reasons for why we do things. Apparently we really believe these reasons. However, in many cases they are not the true causes of our behaviors. It is good to differentiate between **reasons** (the explanations that people make up) and **causes** (the physical, biological things that influence or lead to certain behaviors). Our left hemispheres seek reasons, but scientists seek causes. The left hemisphere seems to be designed to be in charge of interpreting behavior – confabulating reasons to explain behavior.

Whole vs. Parts

The major findings of split-brain research can be summarized as follows: The left hemisphere is usually better at language, logic, analysis, and noticing details. The right hemisphere excels at holistic perception, patterns, orienting, spatial tasks, and emotions. If we give a split-brain patient a jigsaw puzzle to solve, her right hand (controlled by the left hemisphere) is terrible at it, but her left hand (right hemisphere) solves it right away. A verbal problem, on the other hand, would be solved much easier by the left hemisphere than by the right. A person who has a stroke or suffers damage by any cause to the left hemisphere will have difficulty with language, analyzing, and logical reasoning. Damage to the right hemisphere leads to problems in spatial perception, emotional reactions, and making sense of data holistically.

Another difference is also apparent: If we show a split-brain patient a picture of a face that is made of vegetables, what will the person report seeing – the face or the vegetables? It depends on which hemisphere sees the image! The left hemisphere focuses best on parts or details, so if we put the image in the right field of vision (seen by the left hemisphere) the person will say "vegetables." But, if we put the image in the left field of vision so it is seen by the right hemisphere,

then the person points to the word "face." Right hemispheres are better at recognizing whole patterns; left hemispheres are better at perceiving and analyzing details.

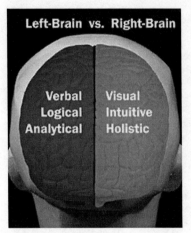

While research has shown that a number of psychological functions are lateralized (better done by one hemisphere than the other), it is important to remember that both hemispheres are involved in nearly all mental processing, particularly complex cognitive functions, and that they work together in coordinating our mental world. Be careful when you read or hear statements about the left and right hemispheres that oversimplify this concept. The hemispheres work together pretty much all the time; it's just that one hemisphere is a bit better than the other at some tasks.

Potentials

A common assumption about brains is that more intelligent people use more brain cells than do less intelligent people. But, in fact, research shows just the opposite. When an adult solves a problem, brain-imaging studies show that people who know the problem well and can solve it easily have less brain activity than people who struggle with it. Perhaps learning results in using fewer brain cells to solve a problem. This is known as **efficiency theory** – the idea that intelligent brains work more efficiently. If you have to use a lot of brain cells to solve a problem, perhaps you're not very familiar with that problem.

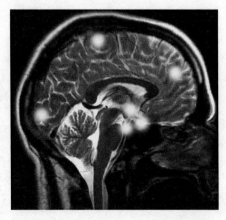

Here's an example of efficiency theory: Math and physics genius Albert Einstein was given an EEG in 1954 and his brain showed normal alpha waves when he solved mathematical problems with which he was familiar. However, when he found a mistake in one of his earlier calculations, his alpha waves suddenly dropped out! Today's researchers find the same thing; when people are good at solving a problem, they use very little of their brain. But a person who is having difficulty with a problem uses a large portion of brain. By the way, Einstein's brain was saved after his death, and it did show some marked anatomical differences from normal brains.

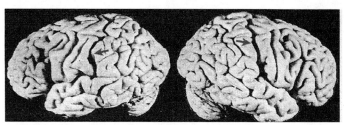

Einstein's brain with arrows showing an unusual formation of the lateral fissure swooping upward.

Finally, here is perhaps the most common question that brain scientists are asked: Is it true that people only use 10% of their brains? Well, the answer is yes, but only during election years!

The true answer might be a bit surprising: It is no. Brain cells are either alive or dead. In that sense, you are always using the cells that are alive. No one seems to know where this fallacy originated, although there are many brain facts that could have inspired this myth. For example, brains consist of billions of cells, so there are a huge number of networks possible, and you're certainly not using all of the potential connections between cells. Also, we can always store more information into our memories; no one is ever full. So, in that sense, too, there is always more potential than we are currently using.

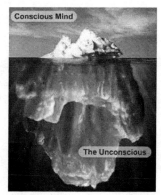

Another possible source of the myth is **Sigmund Freud**'s idea that the conscious part of the human mind makes up only 10% of mental life, while the **unconscious** part accounts for 90%. Freud's notion is part of his theory of **psychoanalysis**, which is very different from modern brain science because Freud postulated stories, thoughts, and wishes as part of the unconscious. However, an interesting coincidence is that some psychologists today have suggested that we are unaware of about 90% of what our brains are doing mentally and cognitively (Bargh & Morsella, 2008). Modern science suggests that our behaviors and mental processes are mostly unconscious.

On the other hand, perhaps what is meant by this myth is that the brain has lots of potential for learning, thinking, and memory storage. That, of course, is very true. The rest of this book will attempt to reveal how great that potential is.

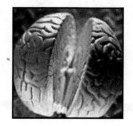

Chapter 7

BRAIN FUNCTIONS
What do all those brain parts do?

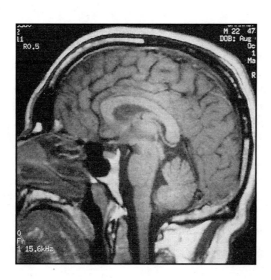

The human brain's cerebrum (the wrinkly part on the top) consists of layers of cells that are organized in columns. The outer, surface layer of the cerebrum is called the **cortex** (from the Latin for "bark"), or more properly, the **cerebral cortex**. Think of it as the skin of the cerebrum. The cerebrum has many wrinkles, which are located roughly in the same places in each of us, though there are some differences from individual to individual (as with fingerprints).

Lobes

Scientists divide the cerebral cortex into various geographic regions, using fissures as the boundaries. Remember, there are both left and right hemispheres of the cerebrum. There are two major fissures on each hemisphere (two on each side). One fissure extends down the hemisphere from the top middle almost vertically. It is called the **central fissure** (sulcus) or the **fissure of Rolando**. Another large fissure extends horizontally from the middle front of the cerebral cortex toward the back. It is called the **lateral fissure** or the **fissure of Sylvius**. So, there is one deep groove that is roughly vertical, the central fissure, and another that is somewhat horizontal, the lateral fissure. These fissures are used as landmarks or boundaries in dividing each hemispheric cortex into four regions called **lobes**.

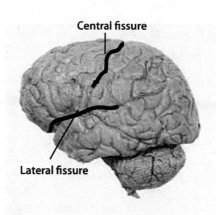

Central fissure

Lateral fissure

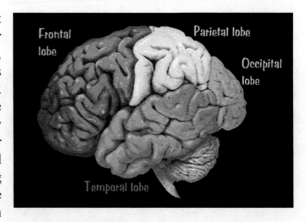

Frontal Lobe: This is the lobe that distinguishes humans from other animals. In humans, it is very large, bulging out in front, and extends from the very front of the head back to the central fissure. The frontal lobe is responsible for purposeful body movements, language and grammar (left side only), and the highest mental functions, including planning, holding things in mind, foreseeing future events, inhibition (restraining us from carrying out our impulses), and other executive functions. It is like the leader, the overseer, or the CEO of the brain. Our working memory (when you hold thoughts in awareness) is generated here. The frontal lobe, more than any other brain region, is responsible for our most human characteristics.

Emotions are also a part of the frontal lobe's functions. In particular, the frontal lobe helps identify emotions and modulates, or helps to regulate, emotional responses generated by activity in the lower, limbic system. The frontal lobe curls down in the front and meets the limbic system, establishing a place where neural pathways can connect the two areas. If you make a fist with your thumb below your fingers, you can get an idea of this arrangement. Your knuckles represent the front of the frontal lobe, and your thumb is the limbic system. The tips of your fingers are the part of the frontal lobe that lies next to the emotional, lower limbic area.

Parietal Lobe: This region is at the top, back of the cerebral cortex. It is a very large lobe that has many functions, including body and skin sensations, pain perception, spatial perception (maps, orientation, depth perception), processing of music, and memories of various kinds. The parietal lobe stores information about where we saw things, and helps us navigate through the environment, acting as a computer for mapping our world. For

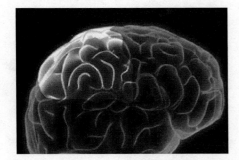

example, damage to the parietal lobe may interfere with orientation in the environment. Our conscious maps of the world and our ability to move around directionally are created and processed by the networks of cells in the parietal lobe.

Visual imagery, body perception, and some forms of mathematics are also among the many functions of this brain region. The parietal lobe contains brain areas specialized for receiving signals from the body which relay information about touch, body motion, pressure on the skin, temperature, and other kinesthetic data.

Occipital Lobe: This is the area at the back, bottom of the cerebral cortex, and is involved with processing and interpreting visual information. The cells in this lobe are organized into networks that process visual information not as a whole, but in parts; that is, visual processing in the occipital lobe is accomplished in parts, or modules. Damage to a specific region of this area will disturb only a particular characteristic of vision, such as seeing movement, color, or shapes, or perceiving diagonal lines,

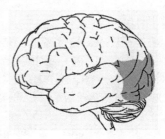

faces, depth, and so on. More brain area is involved in the processing of visual information than for processing any other single function. Visual perception is a complicated business. Damage to the left occipital lobe will disturb vision in the right field of vision, and vice versa.

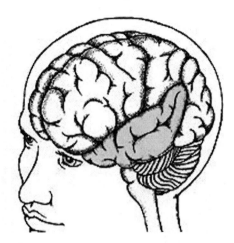

Temporal Lobe: This is the area located below the lateral fissure. One of its main functions is perceiving sounds. Certain areas of the temporal lobe when electrically stimulated cause a person to hear specific sounds. The ears are like the eyes in that the left and right ears each send some information to the left and right hemispheres. That is, the temporal lobe in the left hemisphere receives auditory information from both the left ear and the right ear, and the right temporal lobe receives information from both ears. Therefore, damage to only one temporal lobe will interfere with hearing in both ears.

    The temporal lobe also is involved in identifying objects. For example, a laboratory animal with damage to the temporal lobe will be able to see and move around in the environment, but will not recognize objects that were seen before. The visual processing area of the occipital lobe sends signals to the temporal lobe regarding the identity of objects. While the parietal lobe processes *where* an object was seen, the temporal lobe processes *what* was seen. Another function of the temporal lobe is to understand the meanings of words. Damage in this brain area will *not* interfere very much with grammar or the pronunciation of words (those are frontal lobe functions), but will cause a person to have difficulty comprehending the *meaning* of words.

Localization of Function

    To some extent, the brain is divided into modules that perform specific functions for tasks. This is not the case for all psychological functions, nor is the brain organized according to English language concepts; for sometimes it's difficult to say exactly what the specialty is for a certain brain region. But in some cases, for some psychological functions, the brain does have

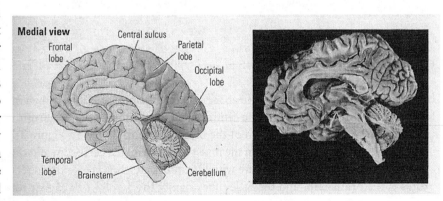

separate (though interacting) modules. This idea that certain mental states and behaviors are controlled by a specific location in the brain is called **localization of function**. Here are some examples:

    1. **Vision** is processed by cells in the occipital lobe. These cells are organized in layers that are labeled V1, V2, V3, and so on. The pathway of visual processing begins with the V1 cells on the surface of the cortex in the back of the brain and then flows forward in the brain, eventually dividing into two pathways.

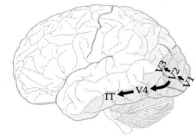

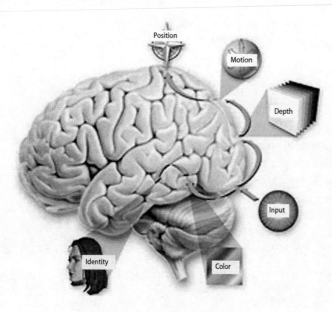

One visual pathway processes and remembers visual information about *what* was seen. This pathway flows into the temporal lobe and is simply called the **what pathway**. The other system of cells carries neural information forward and upward into the parietal lobe and processes and remembers *where* something was seen. This is called, as you might guess, the **where pathway**. The temporal lobe processes information about what is seen, while the parietal lobe computes where it was seen.

Damage in the occipital lobe, naturally, will adversely affect the processing of vision; that is, will lead to some sort of blindness or visual impairment. The particular visual problems that arise from damage in the occipital lobe depend on where the damage occurs. The cells of this area are very specific in their jobs. If the V1 cells (on the surface of the cerebral cortex, at the lower, back of the cerebrum) are damaged, a person will report an inability to see anything in an area of the visual field that is the same shape as the damage in the occipital lobe on the opposite side of the damage. Damage in the left occipital lobe in the shape of a star will result in a blind spot in the right visual field in the shape of a star.

Here's another interesting example: Damage to one area of the visual processing pathway will impair the ability to recognize familiar faces, a condition called **prosopagnosia**. In these cases, people do not recognize even very familiar people by sight; they need other stimuli, such as hearing the person's voice. This condition is caused by damage to a particular region of the brain (on the side, just behind the ear) known as the **fusiform face area** (FFA), a part of the what pathway. The FFA is a specialized area that allows quick recognition and memory of faces, and also is activated when a person becomes an expert at identifying objects visually. For instance, experienced bird watchers use their FFAs to quickly identify birds. Also, near the face area is a brain region that becomes active when a person is visually recognizing bodies. Objects are recognized in a nearby area.

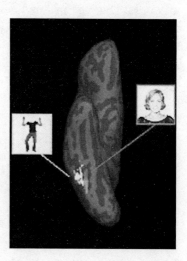

2. **Hearing** is perceived in two areas located in the lateral fissures of the temporal lobes of each hemisphere. Each area is known as a primary **auditory cortex**. The primary auditory cortex is located deep within the fold, or sulcus, just at the top of the temporal lobe on the side of the head. Damage to one of these brain areas, the primary auditory areas, would result in loss of some hearing in both ears because each ear sends some signals to the left and right hemispheres. The neural signals from an ear are mostly contralateral, but partially ipsilateral. That is, messages from an ear go mostly to the opposite hemisphere, but somewhat to the same-side hemisphere.

Primary auditory cortex

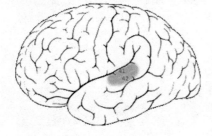

The auditory cortex cells are arranged in layers that interpret the frequency (pitch) of sound. Interestingly, the layers are arranged very much like the keys on a piano. Wilder Penfield was a Canadian brain surgeon who, beginning in the 1930s, gently stimulated patients' brains with an electrode in order to locate the source of their epilepsy. Penfield discovered that the brain is highly localized. When he stimulated one area of the primary auditory cortex, for instance, the patient would hear a violin playing. When the electrical pulse was stopped, the patient said the sound ended. Stimulation of another area would result in the memory of a specific event. When stimulated in the visual area, one patient said, "Robbers are coming at me with guns."

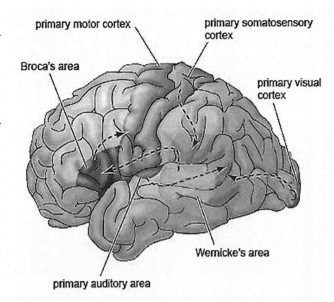

3. **Body Movement** is controlled by a gyrus, or bump, at the top of the cortex, at the very rear of the frontal lobe just in front of the central fissure, extending from the top down, nearly vertically. This area is known as the **motor cortex**, the **motor strip**, or simply the **motor area** (the term "motor" comes from the Latin and means "movement" or "motion"). The cells in this part of the brain send electrical signals to the skeletal muscles, initiating movement of the body. If you want to move your arm, leg, or any part of your body, the cells in this region must be activated. Signals from the primary motor area are sent to lower brain areas where other brain systems add to the neural signals that are sent to the muscles so that movements will be smooth and coordinated.

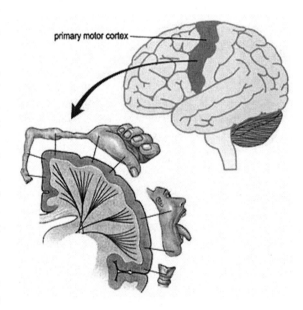

The primary motor area is arranged upside down. That is, the cells at the top of the motor strip send signals to the feet, while the cells at the bottom of the motor strip control movements of the mouth and tongue. Damage to any section of the motor strip will cause difficulties in movement (paralysis) in the corresponding part of the body that the motor area controls. For instance, a person damaged at the top of the motor cortex in the left hemisphere will have paralysis of the right foot. Damage to the middle of the right motor strip will cause paralysis in the left arm.

The primary motor area is connected to other, nearby brain regions that help with planning a movement, or assembling sequences of movement. These are called the premotor area and the supplementary motor area. They lie in front of the primary motor area, which is at the very back of the frontal lobe, one in each hemisphere.

4. **Body Sensation** is processed by the cells in a brain gyrus (bump) just behind the central fissure in the parietal lobe. This brain bump is called the **somatosensory cortex**, **strip**, or **area**. It is located just behind the motor area – the motor area in front, and the touch area behind the central fissure. This place in the brain receives incoming signals from the body via the spinal cord and supports the perception of touch, temperature, body

position, and pain; although, these perceptions are influenced by activation in other brain areas, too. Just as with the motor cortex, the somatosensory cortex is organized upside down. A person injured at the top of this strip in the right hemisphere would have numbness, a lack of feeling, in the left foot.

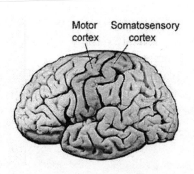

A "homunculus" (small person) is a drawing that illustrates the relative sizes of the subregions of the motor and somatosensory strips associated with different parts of the body (for example, a very big brain region feels the hands an fingers). It was once believed that these subregions of the brain were precisely connected to movements and sensations in specific body parts – that the homunculus was a precise indicator of brain-body connections. However, recent research has shown that the motor and somatosensory strips are much more complicated than previously realized (Helmuth, 2002). For example, a steady stimulation of a region of the motor strip causes a monkey's arm to move to its mouth no matter where the arm was originally positioned. These new findings remind us that we need to use caution in not oversimplifying the brain's organization, plasticity, and complexity of function.

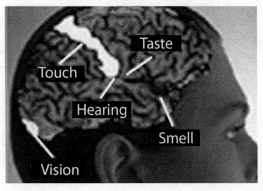

Although the brain regions mentioned above are specialized for certain functions, it is important to remember that brains are dynamic, living organs that are complex, interconnected, and changeable. The sensory systems are in communication with each other and act like instruments in an orchestra – they react to each other and create a symphony through teamwork. Each instrument (brain region) is modulated by other regions. In fact, scientists have found brain cells that receive signals from more than one sense, so called **multisensory** (or **multimodal**) **neurons** (Driver, 1998). For instance, when people touch ridges on a pad that they cannot see, parts of the visual areas of their brains become activated. In fact, disruption of the visual area interferes with feeling the ridges! Similarly, when blind people have activity in their visual areas disrupted, it causes them difficulty in reading Braille by touch.

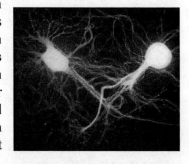

There are many other examples of how the brain coordinates sensory systems. Some researchers now believe that all perception is multisensory (Stoffregen, 2001). When adults had air blown into their faces, watched moving dots on a screen, or listened to sounds on headphones, not only did their touch, vision, and hearing brain areas become more active, but in each case brain activity in three other areas increased (Bremmer, 2001). These brain regions presumably are **cross-sensory**.

The **McGurk effect** is especially weird. When subjects watch a video of a person speaking a syllable, but they hear a different syllable on the sound track, the subjects report hearing a sound that is a combination of the two. For example, if we see a person whose lips are pronouncing, "ga," but we hear the person saying, "ba," then we perceive the sound of "da." Because we can read lips, our visual system is receiving a different message than our auditory system. Therefore, our brains construct a perception that is a combination of the two inputs. Brains are pretty cool perceiving machines!

5. **Language** in most people is processed in the left hemisphere. Most right-handed people have a slightly larger left hemisphere where language abilities are concentrated. Left-handers sometimes process language in the right hemisphere, or in both sides of the brain, but about half of lefties also have their language areas in the left hemisphere.

By language, we do not mean just speech. A parrot that imitates sounds is not using language. Human languages have a structure, a grammar. For example, **syntax** refers to the proper order of words in a sentence. Sentence this not syntax proper have does. Using a grammatical language is a complicated computational problem that requires a large number of brain networks. Amazingly, children all over the world learn language very easily and rapidly no matter the language community in which they are raised. This is because human brains are anatomically evolved to accomplish this wonderful feat. Language is an instinct. This does not mean it is inborn; rather, it means that the proficiency to learn language has evolved genetically within the species.

Two brain regions are critically involved with language. French doctor **Paul Broca** (1824-1880) discovered that an area in the left frontal lobe is important for pronunciation and grammar. This brain area is now called **Broca's area** in his honor. One of Broca's patients was called "Tan" because that was the only word he could say. Tan's brain was damaged in the left frontal lobe, the region now called Broca's area. If a person has damage in this region, say from a **stroke** (an accident in the blood vessels that deprives brain cells of oxygen, typically caused by a blood clot), the person is said to have **Broca's aphasia** or **expressive aphasia**. The term "aphasia" is used to designate any brain problem in the use or understanding of language. In Broca's aphasia, a person will have difficulty pronouncing words and producing correct grammar. Such people

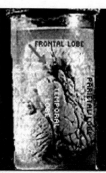

Dr. Paul Broca, and the brain of his patient known as Tan showing damage to the part of the frontal lobe now known as Broca's area.

may sound intellectually impaired because of their slurred speech or improper grammar, but it is important to note that Broca's aphasia does not interfere with intelligence or the understanding of language.

A German doctor, **Carl Wernicke** (pronounced "VER-nih-kee") (1848-1904), discovered another region of the brain involved in language. This area is located further back from Broca's area, in the back of the temporal lobe. This brain region is involved in processing the meaning of words and sentences, and is now called **Wernicke's area**. People with damage in this area are said to have **Wernicke's aphasia** or **receptive aphasia**. Such patients have difficulty understanding language. They may speak in ways that do not make sense, or they may create sentences that are very empty, using "like," "you know," and "whatever" to conceal their lack of understanding.

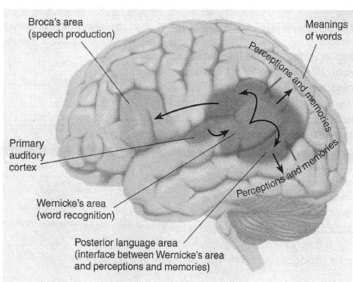

So, Broca's area is primarily an area for the expression or production of language. We use it to create speech, sign language, or when writing a sentence. Wernicke's area is predominantly a receiving or comprehension area for language, used when listening to language or when reading a sentence.

When a person wants to say something, Wernicke's area first creates the meaning of the words. Then Broca's area adds the grammar and pronunciation. Then the motor areas that control the mouth, tongue, and speech apparatus will express the language. The anatomy and physiology of these regions is primarily a matter of heredity, and a healthy human brain will learn language very easily and quickly when exposed to it at the right age. People who learn a second language early in life will use the brain cells in Broca's area for both of their languages. On the other hand, since Broca's area has a critical period, people who learn a second language later in life will have to rely on brain cell networks in regions other than Broca's area. This is why it is so much more difficult to learn another language as an older child or an adult. In most people the left hemisphere is best at processing and expressing language, while the right hemisphere leans toward music, rhythm, and melody. Interestingly, the Chinese language Mandarin uses lots of intonation (for example, a word can have different meanings depending on how it is pronounced), and therefore Mandarin speakers use both hemispheres for language, as compared to English speakers who use predominantly the left (Scott, 2003).

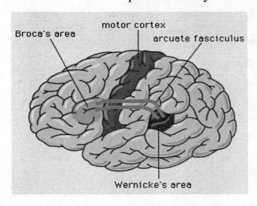

The two language areas are connected below the surface of the cerebrum by a band of cells known as the **arcuate fasciculus**. Via this white bundle, Broca's and Wernicke's areas can communicate and cooperate with each other. Patients with damage to the arcuate fasciculus experience what is called **conduction aphasia**; they have difficulty making an association between the understanding of language and the expression of language. It's a bit like listening to a political press conference – questions are asked and understood, but answers are given that are not related to the questions! There is a lack of communication between reception and expression. Researchers have found higher rates of conduction aphasia in people with schizophrenia and people who smoke marijuana (Ashtari, 2005).

When we want to speak, our brains must coordinate the two language areas. The meaning of what is to be said is pulled together in Wernicke's area and then a signal is sent to Broca's area, which is the sub-computer for grammar and pronunciation. From there the signal goes to the speaking apparatus in the mouth and throat.

Reading is different, of course. When reading we need to transform a visual image into a sound. We need to convert orthography (the letter forms) into phonology (sounds). We see a particular visual shape, like the letter "T," a vertical line with a shorter horizontal line on top, and we think the sound "teh." This transformation happens in the what pathway, the tract of visual cells from the occipital lobe passing to the temporal lobe, the seat of word meanings and identification. One brain area, the **angular gyrus**, seems to play a critical role in this conversion of letter shapes into sounds. Connections are made with other areas of the brain that help form a concept with all the meanings and relationships that a word can have. It has also been found that patients with damage to the angular gyrus in the right hemisphere were unable to grasp the dual meaning of metaphors (Ramachandran, 2004).

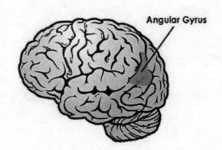

With reading disorders, such as **dyslexia**, the problem is not with a particular part of the brain, but rather with the software pathways in which the signals are processed in a sequence. In order to read efficiently, a number of brain areas must coordinate their processing in a particular, definite order. In dyslexia, the reading signals are not flowing properly from one brain area to the next. The sequence of processing is important, and when it goes awry, then reading problems occur. Brain-imaging studies show clear differences in brain activation patterns between good readers and struggling readers (Shaywitz, 2002).

Dyslexia, however, is a broad term that includes many different reading problems, only some of which involve errors in the sequential processing of language information. That is, problems in reading have many different causes, and the term dyslexia is not consistently used. However, brain research has found clear neural evidence for dyslexia, particularly noting the left upper back of the cerebral cortex, a brain region for phonological processing (Shaywitz, 2006).

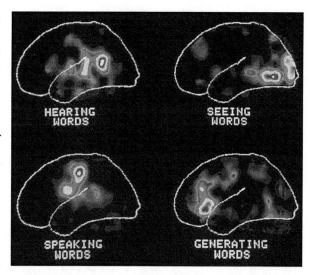

These PET scan images show which areas of the brain are active when a person processes words in four different ways. For example, when hearing words, the auditory area and Wernicke's area in the temporal lobe are active. But, seeing words is associated with activity in the occipital lobe. When we generate, or think up words, the frontal lobe lights up, while speaking requires Broca's area and the motor cortex.

6. One of the topics studied by cognitive psychologists is called **theory of mind**. People understand that other people have mental processes that include thinking, feeling, intentions, and reasoning. As adults, we readily and automatically assume that other people have a mental life; we often can read their intentions, beliefs, knowledge, and emotions from their behaviors. Chimps can do this to some extent, too. Scientific study on this presumption is known as theory of mind research

Theory of mind is a skill that develops early in life. It appears to be genetically innate, but like language, still requires experience for it to develop and flourish. Young children do not show complete development of this cognition. For example, suppose we have a typical three-year-old, Jill. We show Jill a candy box, but when we open it she sees that it is filled with pencils. Now along comes Mike, who did not see the candy box when open. If we ask Jill what Mike thinks is in the candy box, she says, "pencils." She cannot separate her own perceptions, feelings, and thoughts from those of others.

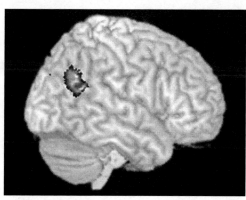

Cognitive neuroscientists who study theory of mind have discovered an area of the cerebral cortex that is active when people think about other people's thoughts (Saxe, 2003). This area is found in the cerebral cortex just where the temporal and parietal lobes meet, and hence is called the **temporoparietal junction**.

This is perhaps the first time that an abstract, complex cognition has been found to be related to a specific brain region. This brain area has also been found to play a role in distinguishing between self and others, a component of social cognition. Also, clinical observations have found that when this area is damaged it tends to produce an out-of-body experience in the affected person.

Mirroring

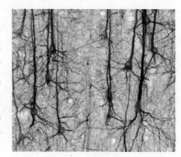

One of the most exciting findings in recent years is the **mirror neuron**. First discovered in monkeys, researchers noticed brain cells that fired when a monkey made a body movement and also when the monkey saw someone else make the same movement. Mirror systems have been found in humans, though the human system seems more widespread in various brain regions than it is in the monkey brain.

Modern brain scientists are currently studying the relationship between mirror neurons and language development (mirror neurons have been found near Broca's area), understanding intentions, empathy (certain brain areas are active when a person feels an emotion and also when seeing another person experience that emotion), theory of mind, and problems such as autism. For example, it has been found that children with autism are less likely to yawn when seeing others yawn (Helt, 2010).

Plasticity

When rats are raised in a complex, enriched environment, their neurons grow more dendrites and create more synapses (Greenough, 1975). In blind individuals who read Braille, the area of the brain that represents the index finger grows in size at the expense of the brain areas devoted to the other fingers (Pascual-Leone, 1993). People who experience damage to one area of the brain often experience compensation as nearby brain areas take over the damaged functions. Even when one hemisphere is damaged, the brain can reorganize so that the other hemisphere assumes tasks such as language and cognition, if the reorganization occurs early enough in life (Guerreiro, 1995).

One of the most common myths about brains is that they are static and unchanging. People are always asking whether some psychological condition is inborn, as if we are stuck with whatever we have at birth. What is inborn is what a baby has at birth. Isn't it obvious that we change? Not only do psychological qualities change over time, but, of

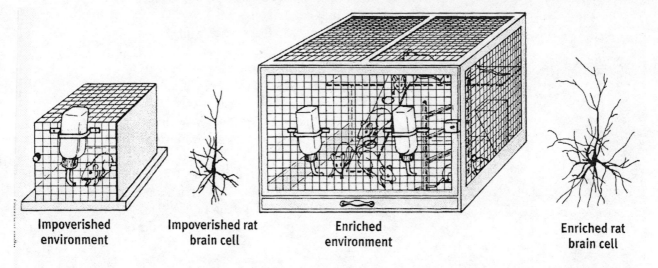

Impoverished environment   Impoverished rat brain cell   Enriched environment   Enriched rat brain cell

course, the source of those traits, the brain, also changes with experience. None of our traits or conditions are inborn; they all develop.

The brain's ability to change is called **plasticity**. Brains are not static, they are dynamic – they change with experience. For example, when people practiced five-finger piano exercises for only five days, researchers found that the area of the brain controlling the fingers was enhanced (Greenfield, 2001). Research by Michael Merzenich (1998) is among the most commonly cited regarding brain plasticity. Merzenich showed that areas of the brain will increase in size with experience. For example, if a monkey is trained to repeatedly touch something with an index finger, the area of the monkey's brain that feels touch in that finger will increase in anatomical size. The number of brain cells used for feeling the index finger will increase.

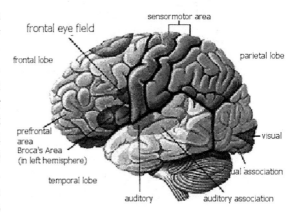

Similarly, brains reorganize in order to process incoming sensory data. When blind people listen to sounds, the cells in their *visual* cortex become active. Deaf people show activity in the *auditory* (hearing) area of the brain when they look at moving dots on a computer screen (Finney, 2001). Apparently the brain recruits cells from other areas in order to help organize incoming information.

Brains are flexible, dynamic organs. To determine just how flexible brain cells are, scientists re-wired the brain of a ferret so that signals from the eyes were diverted to the auditory areas of the brain. Remarkably, the cells of the auditory cortex realigned themselves in a pattern similar to normal visual cells. However, the flexibility was not 100 percent, since the auditory cells did not completely copy the visual cortex. It is wise to remember that nature and nurture work together in an interactive manner.

If a young kitten has one eye blocked for only 24 hours, the cells in the brain that normally receive information from that eye will decrease and the cells that receive information from the other eye will increase (Trachtenberg, 2000). Brain cells change; they are remodeled by experience. Brain and experience are partners.

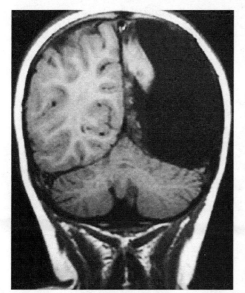

A seven-year old girl had her left hemisphere removed, yet she developed language skills and was able to control the right side of her body to some extent. Brains are quite plastic, particularly in younger people.

Studies of brain plasticity remind us of critical periods, times when biological processes are more responsive to the environment. For example, a baby's brain has the capacity to change, respond, and remodel itself much more than does an adult's brain.

Of course, brains develop over time; the brain of an embryo, or even a newborn, is vastly different from the brain of an adult. And, brain development depends not only on genetics, but on experience in the world. Cells in the eye and in the visual pathway depend on seeing (a newborn blocked from light will not develop normal vision), auditory cells depend on hearing sounds (in fact, noise can interfere with normal auditory cell development; Chang, 2003), learning a language depends on hearing it spoken, and so on.

Phantoms

Another fascinating phenomenon comes from people who have lost a limb. A person whose arm has been amputated, for example, will still feel touch and pain in his or her arm. This experience is called **phantom limb**. The feeling persists even though the limb is not there. A missing arm will itch and hurt. Phantom limb demonstrates that the sense of feeling is not in our limbs, but in our brains! We feel with our brains, not with our body proper. The feeling of a phantom limb is created in the somatosensory area of the cortex. Apparently this brain area is receiving signals from other brain areas about the missing limb. Some research has found that the signals are coming from the frontal lobe (Dingfelder, 2007) and not from nerves in the body.

You can get the feeling of phantom limb by having someone tap you rapidly at the wrist and then the elbow. You may feel a phantom tap in the middle of your arm. This is known as the **cutaneous rabbit illusion** (like a rabbit hopping on your arm). When this was done to volunteers, scans of their brains showed the somatosensory area was active whether the middle of the arm was really tapped or there was just the illusion. So, the feeling is coming from activation of cells in the somatosensory cortex, whether or not the actual limb is being stimulated. In the case of illusionary feelings, perhaps that brain area is being tricked into activation by other brain areas. This research also informs us about how inter-connected, organized, and integrated our brains are.

In the case of phantom limb, another odd thing often occurs. Brain cells in the somatosensory area that are no longer receiving signals from the missing limb, brain cells that are not being stimulated, will begin to make connections with other cells. Brain cells are alive and their job is to receive electrical signals. Brain cells have extensions – branches – that can grow and reach out to make connections with other brain cells. So, if a person's arm is missing, the brain cells that were receiving signals from that arm will then reach out to other cells. The brain cells will reorganize and form connections with nearby cells. The result is that patients will eventually feel their arms when you touch their cheeks! This is because the area of the brain that feels the arm is near the area that feels the face. So, what happens after a while is that a touch on the patient's cheek will activate cells in the somatosensory area that give the person a feeling in his or her arm! The brain cells have organized themselves into a new pattern. This apparently can be reversed: A man who had received a transplanted hand after 4 months experienced a reorganization of his hand's cortical map (Senior, 2001).

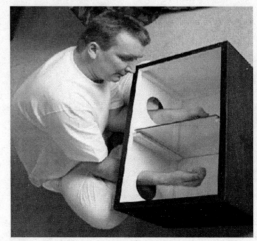

One treatment for people suffering from phantom pain is a **mirror box**. The patient places his or her existing limb in such a position that the missing limb appears in the mirror, the brain can be tricked into thinking the limb is still there using vision. The mirror box sometimes helps relieve pain that often occurs in cases of phantom limb.

Subcortical Areas

Deep inside the brain are a number of interesting areas that together are called **subcortical** because they lie below the cerebral cortex. These brain areas evolved earlier than the cerebral cortex, and therefore are more intimately involved with the activities necessary for day-to-day survival, such as basic emotions, motivations, hunger, sensing the environment, the formation of memories, shifting attention to important stimuli, and maintaining body functions. Here is a list and brief description of some of the most important of these subcortical areas:

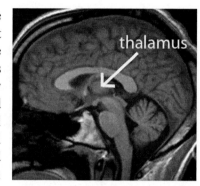

1. About in the middle of the brain is the **thalamus**, a relay center for the senses, and the center of the **limbic system**, a group of brain regions that work together. Sensory processing begins with signals coming into the brain from the eyes, the ears, the tongue, the skin, and from different parts of the body. Before these signals are processed by the cerebral cortex, they first pass through the thalamus where the signals are sorted and distributed to other areas of the brain. There is one exception: The only sensory signal that is received by the cortex first and the thalamus later is smell. All other senses go to the thalamus first. The smell receptors in the nose send electrical signals to a brain area just at the bottom of the frontal lobe known as the **olfactory bulb**. This area represents a large proportion of the brain in some lower animals, but is a relatively small part of a human brain.

The thalamus, then, is a relay center for the senses, much like a train station or airport hub. However, it not only sends signals to various cortical areas for processing, it also receives signals back from the cortex. Some experts believe that this two-way, back-and-forth communication is essential for creating consciousness.

2. An important brain area located just below the thalamus is the "below the thalamus," or the **hypothalamus**. This area acts as a regulator or control center for a number of motivations, such as hunger and thirst. Sometimes the hypothalamus is compared to a thermostat in that it measures bodily functions and then sends signals to the brain in response to those functions. The hypothalamus, for example, measures the amount of sugar in the blood (glucose), and when it is low, sends out the signals that are interpreted as hunger. Another part of the hypothalamus tells us when to stop eating. Thirst works the same way: A section of the hypothalamus measures things like water volume and cellular osmosis (sucking in water) in the body, and when the body cells are dry, the hypothalamus signals the brain. The result is that we feel thirsty. Damage to the hypothalamus, therefore, results in problems with motivations such as hunger and thirst. Damage to the "stop eating" region of a rat's hypothalamus causes the animal to overeat to the point of obesity. In humans, a rare genetic disorder called **Prader-Willi syndrome** causes the hypothalamus to malfunction; sufferers have unending appetites and can even eat themselves to death.

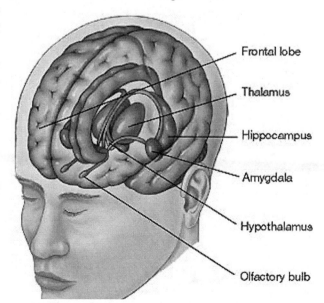

Frontal lobe

Thalamus

Hippocampus

Amygdala

Hypothalamus

Olfactory bulb

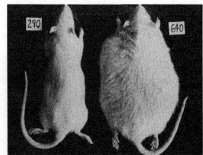

Destruction of the part of the hypothalamus that controls stopping eating made the rat on the right overeat.

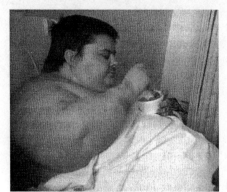

Prader-Willi syndrome causes a person to overeat.

Another region of the hypothalamus is dubbed the **pleasure center**. When electrically stimulated in this area, people say they feel pleasure. Rats with electrodes in this area will push a bar all day long to stimulate these cells. The pleasure center is surrounded by a **pain center**. With electrodes inserted into this brain region, rats will push a bar all day long to avoid receiving stimulation. The hypothalamus has been shown to be involved in many other motivations, such as anger, fear, and sex. An old joke says that the hypothalamus controls the four Fs: fighting, feeding, fleeing, and reproduction.

3. The **pituitary gland** is part of the **endocrine system**, which consists of many glands located throughout the body. Glands are body organs that secrete chemicals called **hormones** into the bloodstream, which then influence the functioning of various body parts and organs. Mood, behavior, and emotions are affected by hormones.

The hormone **oxytocin**, for instance, is known as the "cuddle hormone" because of its role in bonding and social attachment, and the "trust hormone" because people exposed to oxytocin become less fearful and more trusting of others. Another hormone, **vasopressin**, is secreted by the pituitary and influences blood pressure, memory, pair bonding, and aggression.

The endocrine system is not part of the nervous system, but the two systems do work together cooperatively. Many of the glands throughout the body are stimulated by hormones that are released by the pituitary gland in the brain. Therefore, the pituitary has been called the master gland.

The pituitary receives its signals from the brain, principally from the hypothalamus. The pituitary is located just below the hypothalamus, a prime location for the neural connections necessary for signaling the pituitary gland to release hormones. For instance, when people are frightened, the brain signals the hypothalamus, which signals the pituitary, which releases hormones that travel through the bloodstream and influence other glands, such as the adrenal glands, which release adrenalin and other hormones that prepare the body to deal with a dangerous situation. Therefore, the endocrine system is important as a contributor to behavior.

4. The **hippocampus** (Greek for "seahorse," so called because of its curvy shape) bends around in the inside of the temporal lobe and is critically involved in learning and memory, and according to new research, even emotions (Vogel, 2003). The hippocampus is an important area for creating new memories, for recalling memories, for making new brain cells (neurogenesis), and for mapping our environment (spatial memory and navigation). It has been found

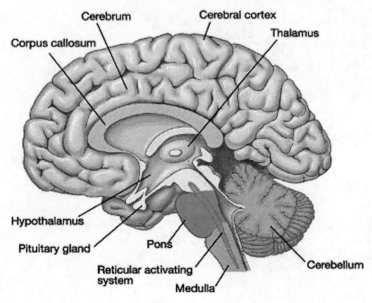

Cerebrum
Cerebral cortex
Thalamus
Corpus callosum
Hypothalamus
Pituitary gland
Pons
Reticular activating system
Medulla
Cerebellum

that taxi drivers in London have large hippocampi, apparently enlarged as maps of the city were stored in the drivers' brains (Maguire, 2000). Lower animals have hippocampal neurons called **place cells** that fire when the animal is in specific location of the environment (O'Keefe, 1978). People suffering from schizophrenia often have smaller hippocampal volume than average, but aerobic exercise increases the volume significantly (Pajonk, 2010). Exercise increases hippocampal volume in people without schizophrenia, too.

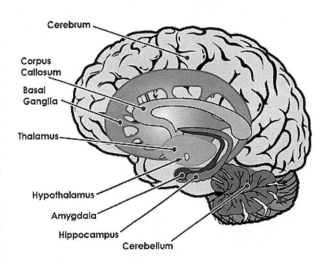

The hippocampi, one on each side of the brain on the inside of the temporal lobe, are part of the **limbic system**, which controls and regulates emotion, motivation, quick reactions to stimuli, memory, and new learning. New cells are created there, too, cells that migrate out to other areas of the brain, such as the frontal lobe, to help program learning and memory into brain circuits. People who are suffering from stress, such as in post-traumatic stress disorder, tend to have smaller hippocampi. Long-term stress reduces the size of the

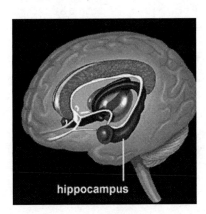

hippocampus and slows learning (Kitayama, 2005). Stress can help an organism adapt in the short-run, but extended stress in the long-run can cause significant damage (Sapolsky, 1997). If you are living a stressful life, please consider making some changes!

When we learn new information, the hippocampus temporarily stores the information, registers it, and then circulates it to other brain areas where memories are created in neural networks. It has been discovered in animals that during sleep the same neurons are firing in the same pattern as when the animal was learning, suggesting that the hippocampus is laying down long-term memories even while asleep (Wilson, 1994). This finding has been replicated repeatedly, and expanded to include humans (Peigneux, 2004). Also, a process called **long-term potentiation** (LTP) has been studied in the hippocampus. It is believed that LTP is one of the main neural processes by which chemical changes at the synapse lead to formation of long-term memories.

When memories are retrieved, the hippocampus helps collect the information from the scattered neural networks in the cortex and other brain regions. Damage to the hippocampus – from alcohol, marijuana, stroke, diseases such as Alzheimer's, or injury – results in **anterograde amnesia**, in which a person has difficulty creating new memories. Movies such as *Memento* (2000) and *50 First Dates* (2004) center on characters with anterograde amnesia.

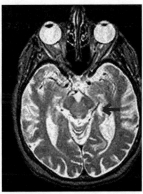

The arrow shows the location of the amygdala.

5. Near the end of the hippocampus is the **amygdala** (Greek for "almond"), which has an oval shape. There is one in each hemisphere. The amygdala is a center for emotions such as fear and anger, and even is important for recognizing facial expressions of emotions. For example, a woman whose amygdalae were both destroyed lost her ability to visually recognize what emotions were being expressed by people's faces, as well as her own ability to express emotions (Damasio, 1994).

Researcher Joseph LeDoux (1996) has traced the formation of an emotional memory in the brains of rats and found that the network of cells involved is in the amygdala. The amygdala is part of the limbic system, as mentioned, a number of coordinated brain parts that lie between the brainstem and the cortex. The limbic system processes emotional feelings and reactions. Signals coming into the brain go first to the limbic system via the thalamus (for a quick reaction without thinking), and then later are processed by the cerebral cortex (for a slower, thoughtful response). For example, if you see a snake in the grass in front of you, the visual information goes to the thalamus and then quickly to the amygdala and surrounding areas of the limbic system, which then alert the body – your heart beats faster, adrenalin flows, blood

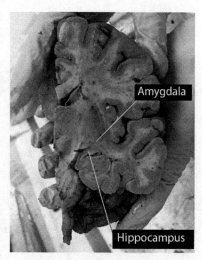

pressure goes up, and so on. But information about the snake also takes another pathway to the cerebral cortex where it is processed by thinking, memory, and judgment. This second avenue (via the cortex) takes longer than the limbic system route because it is more detailed and complex.

So, we have two brain pathways for responding to emotionally charged situations: one quick – the limbic system – for immediate body response to danger, and one slower – the cortex – with more cognitive interpretation (Helmuth, 2003). If you are unexpectedly cut off in traffic, your first response (limbic system) is probably to scream, gesture, and pound on the steering wheel. But, as you process this information with the slower route through the cerebral cortex, you perhaps will become more rational, calmer, and will go about your business. Perhaps you will cognitively explain the experience by telling yourself that the other driver must be in a hurry, has an emergency, has a gun!, or is just a jerk. Your thinking brain helps you modulate an emotional response. But, remember, the emotional response comes first, faster.

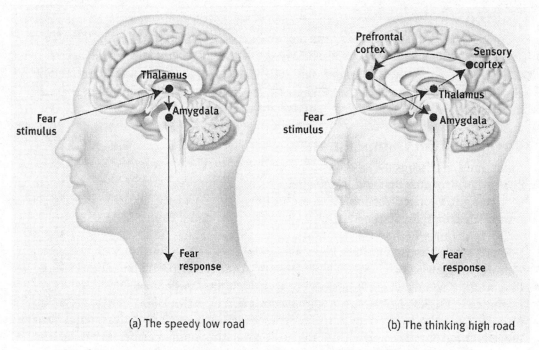

(a) The speedy low road   (b) The thinking high road

When facing danger, the limbic system reacts quickly without thinking. The cortex takes longer to process the information. So, you have a "fight or flight" response that is fast, and then later you think about it.

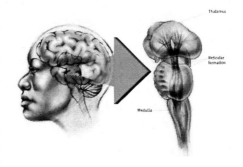

6. The **brainstem** is at the top of the spinal cord. It is the place where brain and spinal cord meet. The brainstem includes a number of nuclei (clusters of brain cells) each responsible for vital body functions necessary for survival and moment-to-moment functioning. For example, the **medulla** (full name = medulla oblongata) controls breathing, heartbeat, blood circulation, and muscle tone. The **pons** is a large bulging section of the brainstem that influences sleep, wakefulness, attention, and arousal. The **reticular formation** is an area that keeps one awake and attentive to things in the environment. Because of its role in "activating" us, the system of nerves that extends up from the brainstem into other brain areas is often called the **reticular activating system** or **RAS**. It can be compared to the channel selector and volume control on a TV set. The RAS determines what we pay attention to and how intense our attention is. There are two general rules for the RAS: First, pay attention to things that are new or different. For example, if something changes in the environment, the RAS in your brain directs your attention to that new, different stimulus. When a stimulus occurs repeatedly, the RAS begins to tune it out; this is called **habituation**.

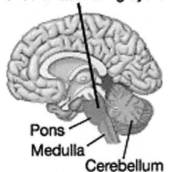

When your brain tires of the sound of your alarm clock, when it is habituated, you need a new alarm clock with a different sound! Psychologists do habituation studies to determine if a baby or animal can distinguish between two stimuli. Expose the subject to one stimulus repeatedly until the response to it is very low, then present the second stimulus. If the response increases, it indicates that the RAS noticed the difference.

Second, things that are meaningful get the attention of the RAS. If you are at a loud party and are concentrating on someone's conversation, and suddenly somewhere else your name is spoken …you will shift your attention to the source of your name. Your RAS responds to things that are meaningful to you. Perhaps you should get an alarm clock that says your name instead of buzzing!

In an habituation experiment, a baby is shown one stimulus until the RAS slows its response to it (as measured by heart rate, looking-time, etc.), then a different stimulus is presented. If the brain's RAS reacts (if the response increases), then the second stimulus was noticed.

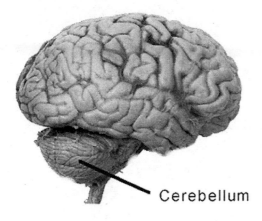

Cerebellum

7. Attached to the back of the brainstem is the **cerebellum** (literally: the little brain), which has a number of jobs as its cells process and store information and communicate with other parts of the brain. One of the jobs of the cerebellum is to store the programs for coordinated body movements. When we practice a movement – playing guitar, golfing, throwing a ball, riding a bike, gymnastics, and other motor skills – the cells of the cerebellum gradually get fused into

a network that will automatically produce the coordinated movement. These coordinated movements do not require thinking; they are performed automatically. Practice may not make perfect, but it does make for cerebellar networks. Damage to these cells of the cerebellum means that a person would need to carefully think about every body movement, as if doing it for the first time, every time.

Also, the cerebellum is important for storing memories of learned body movements. In a famous experiment, a rabbit was taught to blink when a tone sounded and later the researchers found that the memory for this learned reflex was located in the cerebellum of the rabbit. Damaging that area removed the learned response. (Thompson, 1998).

8. Near the thalamus of the brain are a number of centers (nuclei) where neural pathways come together. This set of nuclei are known as the **basal ganglia**, however, this is a bit of a misnomer since the term "ganglia" normally is used for clusters of neurons outside the brain.

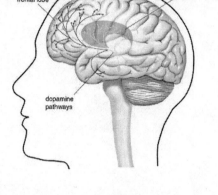

The most studied role of the basal ganglia is control of eye movements. A network of regions converges in an area at the top of the brainstem called the **superior colliculus** where eye movements are centrally regulated. The basal ganglia also help to smooth body movements. Complex movements, like ballet dancing, require smoothing of the movements so we don't jerk at every motion. The cerebellum and basal ganglia work together with the motor cortex to plan, organize, coordinate and smooth our body movements.

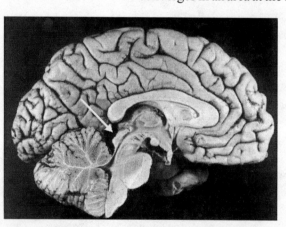

The arrow shows the location of the superior colliculus.

Damage to various areas of the basal ganglia results in a number of different movement disorders, including **dystonia**, **Parkinson's disease**, and **Tourette's syndrome**. In such cases people may have stiff muscles that move or jerk uncontrollably, spasms, tics, or tremors in which the muscles twitch.

Parkinson's disease results from damage to an area of the basal ganglia called the **substantia nigra** that helps produce dopamine in the brain. Sometimes such damage is due to genetics, but injuries, toxins, and infections are just as likely.

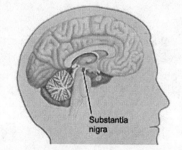

9. The **body's clock** is influenced by a number of brain systems below the cortex. Many aspects of physiology and behavior follow a cycle around day and night – sleep is an obvious example. These are called **circadian rhythms** ("circles around the day"). Many physiological processes (such as blood pressure), moods, and behavior patterns rise and fall at regular intervals during the day. Travelers visiting another time zone often experience jet lag until their body clocks adjust to the new time.

The biological clock is set by incoming light. Certain cells in the eye contain a chemical (melanopsin) that is sensitive to the amount of light illumination (Berson, 2002 & Yau, 2003). These cells send signals to a place in the brain known as the **superchiasmatic nucleus** (above the optic chiasm). This is the main brain region for regulating and setting the daily clock. That is, each day the biological clock is reset by incoming light falling on cells in the back of the eye that connect to the brain. The brain then adjusts body physiology through mechanisms such as the hormone **melatonin** that is released by the pineal gland in the brain. The result of these physiological events is the circadian rhythms of the body.

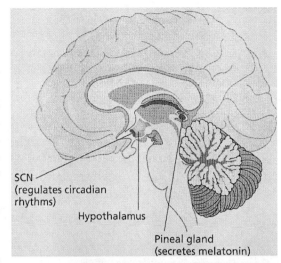

SCN (regulates circadian rhythms)

Hypothalamus

Pineal gland (secretes melatonin)

10. There are several areas of the brain that help to regulate motivation. When we desire a substance or activity, scientists refer to a **reward system** in the brain. This is not one specific region, but rather a collection of brain areas that communicate with each other, often involving certain chemicals within the limbic system. The major role is played by the **mesolimbic pathway**, sometimes called the reward or pleasure pathway. This pathway begins in an area at the top of the brainstem known as the **ventral tegmental area** (VTA) and travels through the limbic system, basal ganglia, and prefrontal cortex, and uses dopamine as a chemical neurotransmitter. In fact, dopamine is produced in the VTA as well as in the substantia nigra.

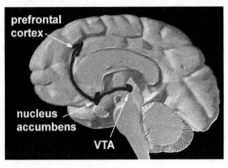

prefrontal cortex

nucleus accumbens

VTA

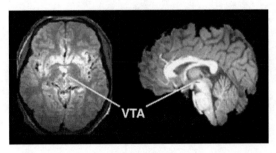

VTA

The VTA is involved in addictions, motivation, cognition, and psychological disorders. Further along the reward pathway, a primary brain region implicated in drug addictions is the **nucleus accumbens**, which is located at the juncture of the frontal lobe and the limbic system. Because of its importance in addiction, one treatment for alcoholism used in China is ablation of this brain area. The nucleus accumbens also processes rewards such as food and sex, is involved in rhythmic timing, and helps regulate emotions induced by music (Menon & Levitin, 2005).

In addition, researchers found lower levels of a chemical called p11 in the nucleus accumbens of depressed patients. The p11 gene helps bring serotonin receptors to the surface of neurons. When the p11 gene is disabled in the nucleus accumbens of laboratory mice, they exhibit behaviors typical of depression. Restoring p11 to that reward area of the brain reversed the depression-like behaviors (Alexander, 2010). The next step is a clinical trial with humans using gene therapy.

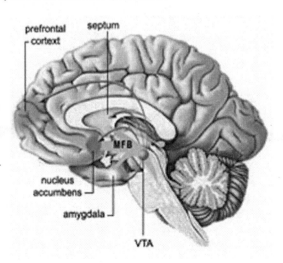

prefrontal cortex

septum

MFB

nucleus accumbens

amygdala

VTA

Conclusion

We have come to the end of our journey through the foundations of psychological neuroscience. The brain, obviously, is a huge topic of study, seemingly endless, and immensely fascinating. Perhaps this book has provided some basic knowledge, and maybe surprised, or even amused you. And, importantly, perhaps this book has whetted your appetite for more information.

A journey through the brain is stimulating, certainly, as you have seen, and sometimes overwhelming. Such information inevitably inspires us to ponder the wonder of it all, the captivating mystery of our brains and minds – self-identity, personality, cognition, intelligence, values, thoughts, beliefs, dreams, and, of course, the enigma of consciousness. Once again we are reminded that the brain really does make one think!

Brain Slice

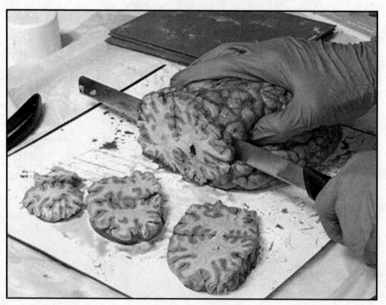

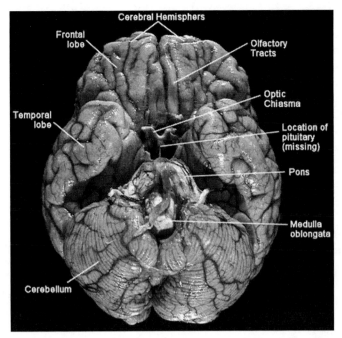

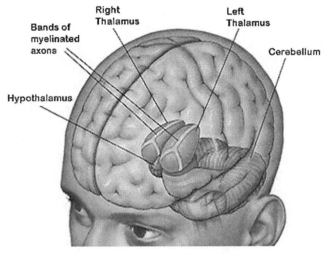

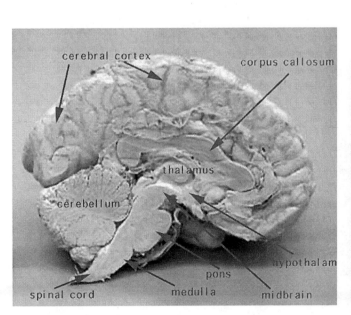

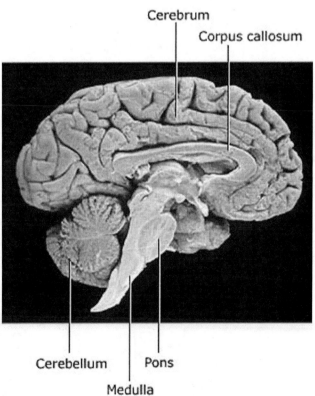

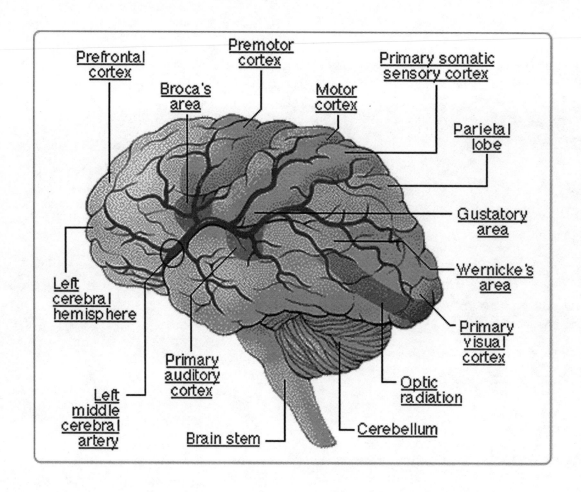

Prefrontal cortex

Premotor cortex

Broca's area

Motor cortex

Primary somatic sensory cortex

Parietal lobe

Gustatory area

Wernicke's area

Left cerebral hemisphere

Primary visual cortex

Primary auditory cortex

Optic radiation

Left middle cerebral artery

Brain stem

Cerebellum

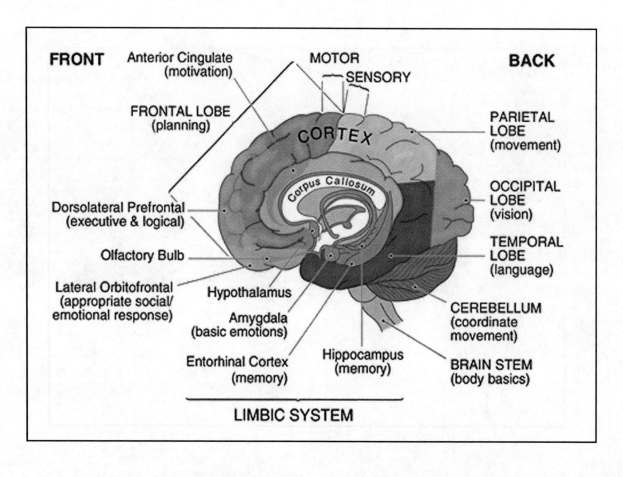

FRONT

Anterior Cingulate (motivation)

MOTOR

SENSORY

BACK

FRONTAL LOBE (planning)

CORTEX

Corpus Callosum

PARIETAL LOBE (movement)

OCCIPITAL LOBE (vision)

Dorsolateral Prefrontal (executive & logical)

TEMPORAL LOBE (language)

Olfactory Bulb

Lateral Orbitofrontal (appropriate social/ emotional response)

Hypothalamus

Amygdala (basic emotions)

Entorhinal Cortex (memory)

Hippocampus (memory)

CEREBELLUM (coordinate movement)

BRAIN STEM (body basics)

LIMBIC SYSTEM

BIBLIOGRAPHY

Adelman, G. (1987) *Encyclopedia of neuroscience*, 2 vols. Boston: Birkhauser.

Alexander, B., Warner-Schmidt, J., Eriksson, T., Tamminga, C., Kaplitt, M. G. et al. (2010). Reversal of depressed behaviors in mice by p11 gene therapy in the nucleus accumbens. *Science Translational Medicine, 2* (54).

Allen, L. S., & Gorski, R. A. (1991). Sexual dimorphism of the anterior commissure and massa intermedia of the human brain. *Journal of Comparative Neurology, 312*:97-104.

Andreasen, N. C. (2001). *Brave new brain: Conquering mental illness in the era of the genome.* New York: Oxford Press.

Arbib, M.A. (1972) *The Metaphorical Brain.* New York: Wiley.

Ashtari, M., Kumra, S., Wu, J., Kane, J., Szeszko, P., & Ardekani, B. (2005). The impact of recurrent exposure to cannabis on brain development in adolescents with schizophrenia and healthy volunteers. *Radiological Society of North America.*

Bargh, J. A., & Morsella, E. (2008). The unconscious mind. *Psychological Science, 3,* 1.

Bellugi, U., et al. Affect, social behavior, and the brain in Williams syndrome. *Current Directions in Psychological Science, 16,* 2, 99-104.

Berson, D. M., Dunn, F. A., & Takao, M. (2002). Phototransduction by retinal ganglion cells that set the circadian clock. *Science, 295,* 1070-1072.

Bertram, L. (2000). Evidence for genetic linkage of Alzheimer's disease to chromosome 10q. *Science, 290,* 5500, 2302.

Biegler, R., McGregor, A., Krebs, J. R., & Healy, S. D. (2001). A larger hippocampus is associated with longer-lasting spatial memory. *Proceedings of the National Academy of Sciences of the United States, 98,* 12, 6941-6944.

Bisiach, E., & Luzzatti, C. (1978). Unilateral neglect of representational space. *Cortex, 14,* 129-133.

Blakemore, C. (1977) *Mechanics of mind.* Cambridge: Cambridge University Press.

Blakemore, C. & Greenfield, S. (1987) *Mindwaves.* Oxford: Basil Blackwell.

Blass, E. M., & Camp, C. A. (2001). The ontogeny of face recognition: Eye contact and sweet taste induce face preference in 9- and 12-week-old human infants. *Developmental Psychology, 37,* 6.

Bontempi, B., Laurent-Demir, C., Destrade, C., & Jaffard, R. (1999). Time-dependent reorganization of brain circuitry underlying long-term memory storage. *Nature, 400,* 671-675.

Brain, L. (1965). *Speech disorders: Aphasia, apraxia, and agnosia.* London: Butterworth.

Brainard, M. S., & Knudsen, E. I. (1998). Experience affects brain development. *American Journal of Psychiatry, 155,* 8, 1000.

Brewer, J. (1998). Making memories: brain activity that predicts how well visual experience will be remembered. *Science, 281,* 5380, 1185-1188.

Brick, J. & Erickson, C. K. (1998). *Drugs, the brain, and behavior: The pharmacology of abuse and dependence.* New York: The Haworth Medical Press.

Buchanan, R. W., Vladar, K., Barta, P., & Pearlson, G. (1998). Structural evaluation of the prefrontal cortex in schizophrenia. *American Journal of Psychiatry, 155,* 8, 1049-1056.

Burdick, K. E., Lencz, T., Funke, B., Finn, C. T., Szeszko, P. R., Kane, J. M., Kucherlapati, R., & Malhotra, A. K. (2006). Genetic variation in DTNBP1 influences general cognitive ability. *Human Molecular Genetics, 15*(10), 1563-68.

Buss, D. M. (1999). *Evolutionary psychology.* Boston: Allyn & Bacon.

Callicott, J. H., et al. (2003). Abnormal fMRI response of the dorsolateral prefrontal cortex in cognitively intact siblings of patients with schizophrenia. *American Journal of Psychiatry, 160,* 4, p. 709-710.

Canli, T., Sivers, H. Whitfield, S. L., Gotlib, I. H., & Gabrieli, J. D. E. (2002). Amygdala response to happy faces as a function of extraversion. *Science, 296,* 2191.

Carmena, J. M., Lebedev, M. A., Crist, R. E., O'Doherty, J. E., Santucci, D. M., Dimitrov, D. F., Patil, P. G., Henriquez, C. S., & Niolelis, M. A. L. (2003). Learning to control a brain-machine interface for reaching and grasping by primates. *Public Library of Science, 1,* Issue 2.

Carter, C. S., Perlstein, W., Ganguli, R., Brar, J., Mintun, M., & Cohen, J. D. (1998). Functional hypofrontality and working memory dysfunction in schizophrenia. *American Journal of Psychiatry, 155,* 9, 1285-1287.

Caspi, A., McClay, J., Moffitt, T. E., Mill, J., Martin, J., Craig, I. W., Taylor, A., & Poulton, R. (2002). Role of genotype in the cycle of violence in maltreated children. *Science, 297,* 5582, 851-854.

Caspi, A., et al. (2003). Influence of life stress on depression: Moderation by a polymorphism in the 5-HTT gene. *Science, 301,* p. 386-389.

Caspi, A., Hariri, A. R., Holmes, A., Uher, R., & Moffitt, T. E. (2010). Genetic sensitivity to the environmant: The case of the serotonin transporter gene and its implications for studying complex diseases and traits. *Amer. J. of Psychiatry, 167,* 509-527.

Chen, E., Cohen, S., & Miller, G. E. (2010). How low socioeconomic status affects 2-year hormonal trajectories in children. *Psychological Science, 21* (1), 31-37.

Churchland, Paul M. (1988) *Matter and consciousness: A contemporary introduction to the philosophy of mind.* Cambridge: MIT Press.

Churchland, Paul M. & Churchland, Patricia Smith (January, 1990) "Could a machine think?" *Scientific American.*

Churchland, P. S. (1986). *Neurophilosophy: Toward a unified science of the mind/brain.* Cambridge: MIT Press.

Colcombe, S., & Kramer, A. F. (2003). Fitness effects on the cognitive funciton of older adults. *Psychological Science, 14,* 125-130.

Crair, M. C., Gillespie, D. C. & Stryker, M. P. (1998). The role of visual experience in the development of columns in cat visual cortex. *Science, 279.*

Crick, F. (1994). *The astonishing hypothesis*. New York: Charles Scribner's Sons.

Crick, F. & Koch, C. (1998). Consciousness and neuroscience. *Cerebral Cortex, 8*, 97-107.

Culbert, K. M., Burt, S. A., McGue, M., Iacono, W. G., & Klump, K. L. (2009). Puberty and the genetic diathesis of disordered eating attitudes and behaviors. *Journal of Abnormal Psychology, 118* (4), 788-796.

Damasio, A. (1994). *Descartes' error*. New York: G. P. Putnam's Sons.

Darwin, C. (1859). *The origin of species*. Cambridge, MA: Harvard University Press.

Dawkins, R. (1976). *The selfish gene*. Oxford: Oxford University Press.

Dennett, D. C. (1991). *Consciousness explained*. Boston: Little, Brown & Co.

Denes, G. (1988). *Perspectives on cognitive neuropsychology*. London: Erlbaum.

Desimone, R. (1991). Face-selective cells in the temporal cortex of monkeys. *Journal of Cognitive Neuroscience, 3*, 1-8.

D'Esposito, M. (1995). The neural basis of the central executive system of working memory. *Nature, 378*, 279-281.

Dingfelder, S. F. (2007). Phantom pain and the brain. *Monitor on Psychology, Jan.*, 22-23

Dimond, S.J., & Beaumont, J.G. (1974). *Hemisphere function in the human brain*. New York: Wiley.

Duncan, J. (2000). A neural basis for general intelligence. *Science, 289*, 5478, 457-463.

Edelman, G. M. (1992). *Bright air, brilliant fire: On the matter of the mind*. New York: Basic Books.

Ellis, A. W., & Young, A. W. (1987). *Human cognitive neuropsychology*. Hillsdale, N. J.: Erlbaum.

Emde, R. N., & Hewitt, J. K. (2001). *Infancy to early childhood: Genetic and environmental influences on developmental change*. New York: Oxford Press.

Ettinger, U. M. (2001). Magnetic resonance imaging of the thalamus in first-episode psychosis. *American Journal of Psychiatry, 158*, 1, 116-118.

Fancher, R. E. (1990). *Pioneers of psychology*, 2nd edition. New York: W. W. Norton.

Feigl, H. (1967). *The "mental" and the "physical."* Minneapolis: University of Minnesota Press.

Fox, N. A., Hane, A. A., & Pine, D. S. (2007). Plasticity for affective neurocircuitry. *Current Directions in Psychological Science, 16*, 1, 1-5.

Fox, P. T. (1986). Mapping human visual cortex with positron emission tomography. *Nature, 323*, 806-809.

Fried, I. (1998). Electric current stimulates laughter. *Nature, 391*, 6668, 650.

Furst, C. (1979). *Origins of the mind: Mind-brain connections*. Englewood Cliffs, NJ: Prentice-Hall.

Gage, F. H., & Kempermann, G. (1999). New nerve cells for the adult brain. *Scientific American, 280*, 5, 48.

Gardner, H. (1985). *The mind's new science: A history of the cognitive revolution*. New York: Basic Books.

Gazzaniga, M. (1985). *The social brain: Discovering the networks of mind*. New York: Basic Books.

Geschwind, N. (1965). Disconnexion syndrome in animals and man. *Brain, 88*, 237-294, 585-644.

Geschwind, N. (1967). Wernicke's contribution to the study of aphasia. *Cortex, 3*, 448-463.

Greenfield, S. A. (1995). *Journey to the centers of the mind*. New York: W. H. Freeman.

Graham-Rowe, D. (2004a). Electrodes on the go. *New Scientist, 13*.

Graham-Rowe, D. (2004b). Brain implants that move. *New Scientist, 25*.

Greenough, W. T. (1975). Experiential modification of the developing brain. *American Scientist, 63*, 37-46.

Griffith, A. (2007). Chipping in: Brain chip for memory repair closes in on live tests. *Scientific American,* February.

Guerreiro, M., Castro-Caldas, A. & Martins, I. P. (1995). Aphasia following right hemisphere lesion in a woman with left hemisphere injury in childhood. *Brain and Language, 49*, 280-288.

Guyton, A. C. (1981). *Textbook of medical physiology*. Philadelphia: Saunders.

Hagerman, R. J. (2002). *Fragile X syndrome: Diagnosis, treatment, and research, 3rd edition*. Johns Hopkins University Press.

Harris, J. R. (1998). *The nurture assumption: Why children turn out the way they do*. New York: The Free Press.

Hebb, D. W., & Penfield, W. (1940). Human behavior after extensive bilateral removals from the frontal lobes. *Archives of Neurology and Psychiatry, 44*, 421-438.

Hebb, D. O. (1949). *The organization of behavior*. New York: Wiley.

Held, R. & Hein, A. (1963). Movement-produced stimulation in the development of visually guided behavior. *Journal of Comparative and Physiological Psychology, 56*, 872-876,

Hellige, J. B. (1993). *Hemispheric asymmetry: What's right and what's left*. Cambridge, MA: Harvard University Press.

Helmuth, L. (2003). Fear and trembling in the amygdala. *Science, 300*, 568-569.

Helmuth, L. (2002). Redrawing the brain's map of the body. *Science, 296*, 1587-1588.

Helt, M. S., Eigsti, I-M., Snyder, P. J., & Fein, D. A. (2010). Contagious yawning in autistic and typical development. *Child Development, 81* (5), 1620-1631.

Henderson, M. (2007). Brain implants could restore speech lost to paralysis. *Brain in the News,* December.

Hertzog, C., Kramer, A. F., Wilson, R. S., & Linderberger, U. (2008). Enrichment effects on adult cognitive development: Can the functional capacity of older adults be preserved and enhanced? *Psychological Science in the Public Interest, 9*, no. 1.

Hinrichs, B. H. (1991). What got into him?: On the causes of human behavior. *Communitas, IV*, 148-153.

Hinrichs, B. H. (1997). Brain research and folk psychology. *The Humanist, 57*, 2, 26-31.

Hinrichs, B. H. (1998). Computing the mind. *The Humanist, 58*, 2, 26-30.

Hinrichs, B. H. (1999). Spiderwebs of silken threads: Memory and the brain. *Communitas, XI*, 10-25.

Hinrichs, B. H. (2001). The science of reading minds. *The Humanist, 60*, 3.

Hinrichs, B. H. (2002). Never mind? *The Humanist, 62*, 1, 36-38.

Hinrichs, B. H. (2005). *Psychology: The essence of a science*. Boston: Allyn & Bacon.

Hinrichs, B. H. (2007). *Mind as mosaic: The robot in the machine*. Minneapolis, Minnesota: Ellipse Publishing Co.

Hinrichs, Bruce H. (2009). *The science of psychology*. Minneapolis: Ellipse Publishing Company.

Hobson, J. A. (1995). *Sleep*. New York: Scientific American Library.

Hobson, J. A. (1996). How the brain goes out of its mind. *Harvard Mental Health Newsletter, 3*.

Hobson, J. A. (2000). Dreaming and the brain: Toward a cognitive neuroscience of conscious states. *Behavioral and Brain Sciences, 23,* 6, 793.

Hoffman, R. E., Boutros, N. N., Hu, S., Berman, R. M., Krystal, J. H., & Charney, D. S. (2000). Transcranial magnetic stimulation and auditory hallucinations in schizophrenia. *The Lancet, 355,* 9209, 1073-1075.

Holland, A. J. (1988). Anorexia nervosa: Evidence for a genetic basis. *Journal of Psychosomatic Research, 32,* 561-571.

Hopkins, W. D., Russell, J. L., & Cantalupo, C. (2007). Neuronanatomical correlates of handedness for tool use in chimpanzees. *Psychological Science, 18, 11,* 971-976.

Hothersall, D. (1984). *History of psychology,* 2nd edition. New York: McGraw-Hill.

Hunt, M. (1993). *The story of psychology.* New York: Doubleday.

James, W. (1890). *Principles of psychology.* New York: Dover.

Klein, D. B. (1970). *A history of scientific psychology.* New York: Basic Books.

Koch, C. (1997). Computation and the single neuron. *Nature, 385,* 6613, 207-211.

Kosslyn, S. M., & Koenig, O. (1992). *Wet mind: The new cognitive neuroscience.* New York: Free Press.

Kosslyn, S. M. (1984) *Ghosts in the mind's machine.* New York: Norton.

Kurzweil, R. (1990) *The age of intelligent machines.* Cambridge: MIT Press.

Kurzweil, R. (1999) *The age of spiritual machines.* New York: Penguin Books.

Kurzweil, R. (2005) *The singularity is near; When humans transcend biology.* New York: Penguin Books.

Lai, C. S., Fishere, S. E., Hurst, J. A., Vargha-Khadem, F., & Monaco, A. P. (2001). A forkhead-domain gene is mutated in a severe speech and language disorder. *Nature, 413,* 519-523.

Larsen, H., van der Zwaluw, C. S., et al. (2010). A variable-number-of-tandem-repeats polymorphism in the dopamine D4 receptor gene affects social adaptation of alcohol use: Investigation of a gene-environment interaction. *Psychological Science, 21* (8), 1064-1068.

LeDoux, J.E. (1996). *The emotional brain: The mysterious underpinnings of emotional life.* New York: Simon & Schuster.

LeGrand, R., Mondloch, C. J., Maurer, D., & Brent, H. P. (2004). Impairment in holistic face processing following early visual deprivation. *Psychological Science, 15,* no. 11, p. 762-768.

Linas, R. (1999). The squid giant synapse: A model for chemical transmission. New York: Oxford University Press.

Llinás, R., & Churchland, P. S. (Eds.) (1998). *The mind-brain continuum: Sensory processes.* Cambridge, MA: MIT Press.

Lykken, D. (1993). Heritability of interests: A twin study. *Journal of Applied Psychology, 78,* 649-661.

Maess, B. Koelsch, S., Gunter, T. C., & Friederici, A. D. (2001). Musical syntax is processed in Broca's area: an MEG study. *Nature Neuroscience, 4,* 540 - 545.

Maguire, E. A., Burgess, N., Donnett, J., Frackowiak, S. J., Frith, C., & O'Keefe, J. (1998). Knowing where and getting there: a human navigation network. *Science, 280,* 5365, 921-925.

Maguire, E. A., et al. (2000). Navigation-related structural change in the hippocampi of taxi drivers. *Proceedings of the National Academy of Sciences of the United States, 97(8),* 4398-4403.

Maxwell, M. L., & Savage, C. W. (Eds.) (1989). *Science, mind, and psychology.* Lanham, Maryland: University Press of America.

McCorduck, P. (1972) *Machines who think.* New York: W.H. Freeman.

Menon, V. & Levitin, D. J. (2005). The rewards of music listening: Response and physiological connectivity of themesolimbic system. *NeuroImage 28(1),* 175-184.

Merzenich, M. (1998). Long-term change of mind. *Science, 282,* 5391, 1062.

Miller, G. (1956). The magic number seven, plus or minus two: Some limits on our capacity for processing information. *Psychological Review, 63,* 81-97.

Milner, B. (1968). Further analysis of the hippocampal amnesic syndrome: 14-year follow-up study of H. M. *Neuropsychologia, 6,* 215-234.

Mishkin, M., & Appenzeller, T. (1987). The anatomy of memory. *Scientific American, 256,* 80-89.

Moises, H. W., Zoega, T., & Gottesman, I. I. (2002). The glial growth factors deficiency and synaptic destabilization hypothesis of schizophrenia. *BMC Psychiatry, 2* (8).

Nisbett, R. E. (1972). Hunger, obesity, and the ventromedial hypothalamus. *Psychological Review, 79,* 433-453.

Norretranders, T. (1998). *The user illusion: Cutting consciousness down to size.* New York: Viking Press.

Ochsner, K. N., & Lieberman, M. D. (2001). The emergence of social cognitive neuroscience. *American Psychologist, 56,* 9, 717-734.

O'Keefe, J. & Nadel, L. (1978). *The hippocampus as a cognitive map.* Oxford University Press.

Olds, J. M., & Milner, P. M. (1954). Positive reinforcement produced by electrical stimulation of septal area and other regions of rat brain. *Journal of Comparative and Physiological Psychology, 47,* 419- 427.

Olton, D.S. (1979). Mazes, maps and memory. *American Psychologist, 34,* 583-596.

Orton, S. (Ed.) (1934). *Localization of function in the cerebral cortex.* Baltimore: Williams & Wilkins.

Pajonk, F-G., et al. (2010). Hippocampal plasticity in response to exercise in schizophrenia. *Archives of General Psychiatry, 67* (2), 133-143.

Pantel, J., Kratz, B., Essig, M., & Schröder, J. (2003). Parahippocampal volume deficits in subjects with aging-associated cognitive decline. *American Journal of Psycbiatry, 160.*

Park, D. C., & Huang, C-M.(2010). Culture wires the brain: A cognitive neuroscience perspective. *Psychological Science, 5* (4), 391-400.

Peigneux, P., Laureys, S., Fuchs, S., et al. (2004). Are spatial memories strengthened in the human hippocampus during slow wave sleep? *Neuron 44(3),* 535-545.

Pascual-Leone, A. & Torres, F. (1993). Plasticity of the sensorimotor cortex representation of the reading finger in Braille readers. *Brain, 116,* 39-52.

Patoine, B. (2005). Rethinking the synapse. *Brain Work, 15,* 6.

Penfield, W., & Perot, P. (1963). The brain's record of auditory and visual experience. *Brain, 86*, 595-696.

Penfield, W., & Rasmussen, T. (1950). *The cerebral cortex of man: A clinical study of localization of function.* New York: Macmillan.

Penfield, W., & Roberts, L. (1959). *Speech and brain-mechanisms.* Princeton: Princeton University Press.

Philibert, R. A., Beach, S. R. H., Gunter, T. D., et al. (2009). The effect of smoking on MAOA promoter methylation in DNA prepared from lymphoblasts and whole blood. *Amer. J. of Medical Genetics, 153B (2)*, 619-628.

Philibert, R. A., Sandhu, H., Hollenbeck, N., Gunter, T., Adams, W., & Madan, A. (2008). The relationship of 5HTT methylation and genotype on mRNA expression and liability to major depression and alcohol dependence in subjects from the Iowa Adoption Studies. *Amer. J. of Medical Genetics, 147B, (5)* 543-549.

Pinker, S. (Ed.) (1985). *Visual cognition.* Cambridge, MA: MIT Press.

Pinker, S. (1997). *How the mind works.* New York: W. W. Norton.

Pinker, S. (2000). *The language instinct: How the mind creates language.* New York: Harper Collins.

Plomin, R. (1990). *Nature and nurture: An introduction to human behavioral genetics.* Pacific Grove, CA: Brooks/Cole.

Posner, N. I., & Raichle, M. (1994). *Images of mind.* New York: Freeman.

Pribram, K. (1971). *Languages of the brain.* Englewood Cliffs, NJ: Prentice-Hall.

Pridmore, S., Bruno, R., Turnier-Shea, Y., Reid, P., & Rybak, M. (2000). Comparison of unlimited numbers of rapid transcranial magnetic stimulation (rTMS) and ECT treatment sessions in major depressive episode. *Int. J. Neuropsychopharmacology, 3* (2), 129-134.

Ramachandran, V. S., 2004. *A brief tour of human consciousness.* Pi Press.

Rauschecker, J. P., & Shannon, R. V. (2002). Sending sound to the brain. *Science, 295*, 1025-1029.

Ray, O. & Ksir, C. (2002). *Drugs, society, and human behavior.* Boston: McGraw-Hill.

Robinson, D. N. (1986*). An intellectual history of psychology.* Madison, WI: University of Wisconsin Press.

Rumelhart, D., & McClelland, J. L. (1986). *Parallel distributed processing: Explorations in the microstructure of cognition*, 2 vols. Cambridge: MIT Press.

Ryle, G. (1949). *The concept of mind.* London: Hutchinson.

Sacks, O. (1985). *The man who mistook his wife for a hat.* New York: Harper & Row.

Sacks, O. (1995). *An anthropologist on mars.* New York: Knopf.

Sacks, O. (2010). *The mind's eye.* New York: Knopf.

Sagan, C. (1979). *Broca's brain.* New York: Random House.

Sagan, C. (1996). *The demon-haunted world.* New York: Random House.

Santarelli, L., Saxe, M., Gross, C., Surget, A., Battaglia, F., Dulawa, S., Weisstaub, N., Lee, J., Duman, R., Arancio, O., Belzung, C., & Hen, R. (2003). Requirement of hippocampal neurogenesis for the behavioral effects of antidepressants. *Science, 301*, 805-809.

Sapolsky, R. M. (1992). *Stress, the aging brain, and the mechanisms of neuron death.* Cambridge, MA: MIT Press.

Sapolsky, R. M. (1996). Why stress is bad for your brain. *Science, 273*, 749-750.

Sapolsky, R. M. (1997). *Why zebras don't get ulcers.* New York: Freeman.

Saxe, R., & Kanwisher, N. (2003). People thinking about thinking people- fMRI studies of Theory of Mind. *Neuroimage.*

Scharff, C. (2000). New neuronal growth in the zebra finch. *Neuron.*

Schlechter, T. M., & Toglia, M. P. (Eds.) (1985). *New directions in cognitive science.* Norwood, NJ: Ablex.

Scott, S. (2003). Brain images of Mandarin speakers. London science exhibit: *British Royal Society.*

Segal, N. L. (1999). *Entwined lives: Twins and what they tell us about human behavior.* NY: Dutton/Penguin Books.

Seidenbecher, T., Rao Laxmi, T., Stork, O., & Pape, H-C. (2003). Amygdalar and hippocampal theta rhythm synchronization during fear memory retrieval. *Science, 301*, 846-850.

Selye, H. (1976). *The stress of life.* New York: McGraw-Hill.

Shean, G. (1978). *Schizophrenia: An introduction to research and theory.* Cambridge, MA: Winthrop.

Shaw, S. H., Mroczkowski-Parker, Z., Shekhtman, T., Alexander, M., Remick, R. A., Sadovnick, A. D., McElroy, S. L., Keck Jr., P. E., & Kelsoe, J. R. (2003). Linkage of a bipolar disorder susceptibility locus to human chromosome 13q32 in a new pedigree series. *Molecular Psychiatry, 8*, 5.

Shaywitz, S. E., Mody, M., & Shaywitz, B. A. (2006). Neural mechanisms in dyslexia. *Current Directions in Psychological Science, 15*, 6, 278-282.

Shaywitz, B., Shaywitz, S., Pugh, K., Mencl, W., Fulbright, R., Skudlarski, P., et al. (2002). Disruption of posterior brain systems for reading in children with developmental dyslexia. *Biological Psychiatry, 52*, 101–110.

Sheline, Y. I., Gado, M. H., & Kraemer, H. C. (2003). Untreated depression and hippocampal volume loss. *American Journal of Psychiatry, 160*: 8,. 1516 – 1518.

Shore, R. (1997). *Rethinking the Brain: New Insights into Early Development.* New York, NY: Families and Work Institute.

Shors, T. J. (2001). Neurogenesis in the adult is involved in the formation of trace memories. *Nature, 410*, 372-375.

Shorter, E. (1997). *A history of psychiatry.* New York: John Wiley.

Shreeve, J. (1995). The brain that misplaced its body. *Discover.*

Silverman, D. H. S., et al. (2001). Positron emission tomography in evaluation of dementia: Regional brain metabolism and long-term outcome. *The Journal of the American Medical Association, 286*, 17, 2120.

Siok, W. T. et al. *(2008).* A structural–functional basis for dyslexia in the cortex of Chinese readers. *Proc. Natl Acad. Sci. USA* 105, 5561-5566.

Skotko, B. G., et al. (2004). Puzzling thoughts for H.M.: Can new semantic information be anchored to old semantic memories? *Neuropsychology, 18*, 4, 756-769.

Sperry, R. W. (1968). Hemisphere disconnection and unity of conscious experience. *American Psychologist, 29*, 723-733.

Springer, S. P., & Deutsch, G. (1998). *Left brain, right brain: Perspectives from cognitive neuroscience*, 5th ed. New York: Freeman.

Squire, L. (1987). *Memory and brain*. New York: Oxford University Press.

Stephan, K. E., Marshall, J. C., Friston, K. J., Rowe, J. B., Ritzl, A., Zilles, K., & Fink, G. R. (2003). Lateralized cognitive processes and lateralized task control in the human brain. *Science, 301*, 384-386.

Stickgold, R., Hobson, J. A., Fosse, R., & Fosse, M. (2001). Sleep, learning, and dreams: Off-line memory reprocessing. *Science, 294*, 1052-1057.

Suppes, P., & Han, B. (2000). Brain-wave representation of words by superposition of a few sine waves. *Proceedings of the National Academy of Sciences of the United States, 97*, 8739-8743.

Swaminathan, N. (2007). The birth of a brain cell: Scientists witness neurogenesis. *Scientific American,* November 9.

Talan, J. (2003, August 19). A gene therapy for the brain. *Newsday (New York),* p. A35.

Talwar, S. K., Xu, S., Hawley, E. S., Weiss, S. A., Moxon, K. A., & Chapin, J. K. (2002). Behavioural neuroscience: Rat navigation guided by remote control. *Nature 417,* 37 – 38.

Thoma, R. J., et al. (2010). Adolescent substance abuse: The effects of alcohol and marijuana on neuropsychological performance. Alcoholism: Clinical and Experimental Research, no. doi: 10.1111/j.1520-0277.2010.01320.x

Thomas, M. S. C. & Johnson, M. H. (2008). New advances in understanding sensitive periods in brain development. *Psychological Science, 17, 1.*

Thompson R.F., Thompson J.K., Kim J.J., Krupa D.J., Shinkman P.G. (1998). The nature of reinforcement in cerebellar learning. *Neurobiol. Learn. Mem. 70,* 150–176.

Thompson, P. M., Cannon, T. D., Narr, K. L., Van Erp, T., Poutanen, V-P., Huttunen, M., Lönnqvist, J., Standertskjöld-Nordenstam, C-G., Kaprio, J., Khaledy, M., Dail, R., Zoumalan, C. I., & Toga, A. W. (2001). Genetic influences on brain structure. *Nature Neuroscience, 4,* 1253-1258.

Trachtenberg, J.T., Trepel, C., Stryker, M.P. (2000). Rapid extragranular in the absence of thalamocortical plasticity in the developing primary visual cortex. *Science, 287,* 2029-2032.

Ullian, E. M. (2001). Control of synapse number by glia. *Science, 291,* 657-660.

Umilitá, M. A., Kohler, E., Gallese, V., Fogassi, L., Fadiga, L., Keysers, C., & Rizzolatti, G. (2001). I know what you are doing: A neurophysiological study. *Neuron, 31,* 1, 155-165.

Ungerleider, L. G. (1995). Functional brain imaging studies of cortical mechanisms for memory. *Science, 270,* 769-775.

Ungerleider, L. G., & Haxby, J. V. (1994). What and where in the human brain. *Current Opinion in Neurology, 4,* 157-165.

Van Turennout, M., Hagoort, P., & Brown, C. M. (1998). Brain activity during speaking: From syntax to phonology in 40 milliseconds. *Science, 280,* 5363, 572-575.

Vargha-Khadem, F., Gadian, D. G., Watkins, K. E., Connelly, A., Van Paesschen, W., & Mishkin, M. (1997). Differential effects of early hippocampal pathology on episodic and semantic memory. *Science, 277,* 5324, 376-381.

Von Neumann, J. (1958). *The computer and the brain.* New Haven, CT: Yale University Press.

Vuoksimaa, E., Kaprio, J., Kremen, W. S., Hokkanen, L., Viken, R. J., Tuulio-Henriksson, A., & Rose, R. J. (2010). Having a male co-twin masculinizes mental rotation performance in females. *Psychological Science, 21* (8), 1069-1071.

Wang, C., Salam, M. T., Islam, T., Wenten, M,, Gauderman, W. J., & Gilliland, F. D. (2008). Effects of in utero and childhood tobacco smoke exposure and beta2-adrenergic receptor genotype on childhood asthma and wheezing. *Pediatrics., 122*(1), 107-114.

Widman, L. E., Loparo, K. A. & Nielsen, N. R., (Eds.) (1989). *Artificial intelligence, simulation, and modeling.* New York: John Wiley & Sons.

Wilson, E. (1979). *The mental as physical.* London: Routledge & Kegan Paul.

Wilson, E. O. (1998). *Consilience: The unity of knowledge.* New York: Alfred Knopf.

Young, J.Z. (1978). *Programs of the brain.* Oxford: Oxford University Press.

Young, R. M. (1970). *Mind, brain and adaptation in the nineteenth century.* Oxford: Clarendon Press.

Zilboorg, G. & Henry, G. W. (1941) *A history of medical psychology.* New York: Norton.

Zuckerman, M. (1991). *Psychobiology of personality.* Cambridge, MA: Cambridge University Press.

INDEX

psychoactive drugs 77
psychoanalysis 93
psychological neuroscience 33
psychosurgery 30
R
radioactive tracers 48
Ramón y Cajal, Santiago 27, 67
receptor 69
recessive gene 59
REM sleep 46
repetitive transcranial magnetic stimulation (rTMS) 51
resting potential 70
reticular activating system (RAS) 111
reticular formation 111
retina 88
reuptake 74
reuptake inhibitors 74.77
reward pathway 113
S
Sacks, Oliver 31
Sagan, Carl 31
schizophrenia 64, 75, 86
seizure 71, 82
selective serotonin reuptake inhibitor (SSRI) 74
semi-identical twins 56
sensitive period (see also: critical period) 38
serotonin 73, 75-76
serotonin syndrome 76
sex chromosomes 54, 59-60
sex-linked chromosomes 60
Sherrington, Charles 25
shock treatment 30, 51
singularity 9
SISCOM 49
slow wave sleep 46
social neuroscience 33
sodium pump 70
soma 67
somatic nervous system 79
somatosensory area 99-100
spatial resolution 47
SPECT 49
sperm cell 53
Sperry, Roger 32
spinal cord 81
split-brain 82-83, 86-92
SQUID 47
SSRI medications 74
stress 43, 44, 62, 68, 76, 109
stroke 101
strychnine 73
subcortical 107
substantia nigra 75, 112
sulci 80
superchiasmatic nucleus 113

superfemale 60
superior colliculus 112
supermale 60
sympathetic division 80
synapse 29, 69, 72-77
synaptic gap (cleft) 72
synaptic transmission 72-73
syntax 101
T
Tan 101
tardive dyskinesia 75
teenage brain 39-42
temporoparietal junction 103
teratogen 64
terminals 68
testosterone 85
thalamus 107
theory of mind 103
theta waves 46
threshold 70
time resolution 47
tomogram 48
Tourette's syndrome 112
transcranial magnetic stimulation (TMS) 51
transcription factors 61
transgenic mice 65
transporters 74
trepanning (trephining) 19
triplet (trinucleotide) repeat 58, 59
Turner's syndrome 60-61
U
unconscious 93
V
vanishing twin syndrome 57
vasopressin 108
ventral tegmental area (VTA) 113
vesicles 72, 73
vision 97-98
visuospatial processes 84
W
Warwick, Kevin 9
Wernicke, Carl 29, 101
Wernicke's area 29, 101
what pathway 98
where pathway 98
white matter 40, 71
Williams syndrome 58-59
Wundt, Wilhelm 28
X
X chromosome 54, 59-60
X-linked 60
Y
Y chromosome 54, 59-60
Z
zygote 55

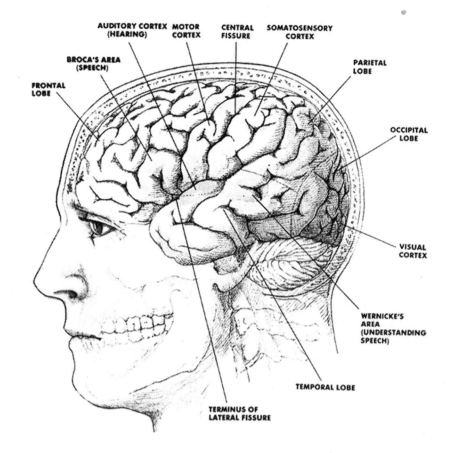

AUDITORY CORTEX (HEARING)
MOTOR CORTEX
CENTRAL FISSURE
SOMATOSENSORY CORTEX
BROCA'S AREA (SPEECH)
PARIETAL LOBE
FRONTAL LOBE
OCCIPITAL LOBE
VISUAL CORTEX
WERNICKE'S AREA (UNDERSTANDING SPEECH)
TEMPORAL LOBE
TERMINUS OF LATERAL FISSURE

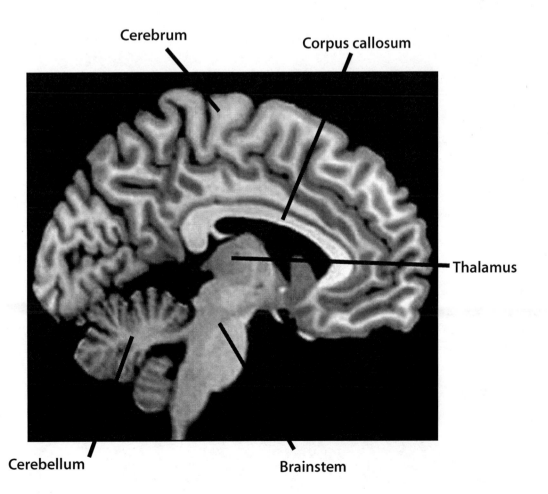

Cerebrum
Corpus callosum
Thalamus
Cerebellum
Brainstem